# It's Hard to Say

Photo @Michael Malyszko, 2013

# It's Hard to Say

SELECTED POEMS

Mary Jo Salter

WAYWISER

First published in the UK in 2015 by

# THE WAYWISER PRESS

Christmas Cottage, Church Enstone, Chipping Norton, Oxfordshire OX7 4NN, UK
P.O. Box 6205, Baltimore, MD 21206, USA
http://waywiser-press.com

Editor-in-Chief
Philip Hoy

Senior American Editor
Joseph Harrison

Associate Editors
Dora Malech | Eric McHenry | V. Penelope Pelizzon | Clive Watkins | Greg Williamson

The poems in this collection originally appeared in the following works:

*Henry Purcell in Japan,* copyright © 1984 by Mary Jo Salter
*Unfinished Painting,* copyright © 1989 by Mary Jo Salter
*Sunday Skaters,* copyright © 1994 by Mary Jo Salter
*A Kiss in Space,* copyright © 1999 by Mary Jo Salter
*Open Shutters,* copyright © 2003 by Mary Jo Salter
*A Phone Call to the Future,* copyright © 2008 by Mary Jo Salter
*Nothing by Design,* copyright © 2013 by Mary Jo Salter

This edition published by arrangement with Alfred A. Knopf, an imprint of
The Knopf Doubleday Group, a division of Random House, LLC.

A CIP catalogue record for this book is available from the British Library

ISBN 978-1-904130-76-5

Printed and bound by
T. J. International Ltd., Padstow, Cornwall, PL28 8RW

*for*

Jean McGarry

# Contents

# Contents

# Contents

## *from* A Phone Call to the Future (2008)

## *from* Nothing by Design (2013)

*from*

# Henry Purcell in Japan

(1985)

# Refrain

*But let his disposition have that scope*
*As dotage gives it.*

– Goneril to Albany

Never afflict yourself to know the cause,
said Goneril, her mind already set.
No one can tell us who her mother was

or, knowing, could account then by the laws
of nurture for so false and hard a heart.
Never afflict yourself to know the cause

of Lear's undoing: if without a pause
he shunned Cordelia, as soon he saw the fault.
No one can tell us who her mother was,

but here's a pretty reason seven stars
are seven stars: because they are not eight.
Never afflict yourself to know the cause –

like servants, even one's superfluous.
The King makes a good fool: the Fool is right.
No one can tell him who his mother was

when woman's water-drops are all he has
against the storm, and daughters cast him out.
Never afflict yourself to know the cause;
no one can tell you who your mother was.

# Two Pigeons

They've perched for hours
on that window-ledge, scarcely
moving. Beak to beak,

a matched set, they differ
almost imperceptibly –
like salt and pepper shakers.

It's an event when they tuck
(simultaneously) their pinpoint
heads into lavender vests

of fat. But reminiscent
of clock hands blandly
turning because they must

have turned – somehow, they've
taken on the grave,
small-eyed aspect of monks

hooded in conferences
so intimate nothing need
be said. If some are chuckling

in the park, earning
their bread, these are content
to let the dark engulf them –

it's all the human
imagination can fathom,
how single-mindedly

mindless two silhouettes
stand in a window thick
as milk glass. They appear

never to have fed on
anything else when they stir
all of a sudden to peck

savagely, for love
or hygiene, at the grimy
feathers of the other;

but when they resume
their places, the shift
is one only a painter

or a barber (prodding a chin
back into position)
would be likely to notice.

# At City Hall

"What kind of license you looking for?"
the woman lounging behind
the counter asked. What *kind*?
A question so disarming the groom

( just outvoicing the dusty carriage
wheels of ceiling fans)
conceded ignorance. "Don't mind
him," the bride said. "A marriage

license." Across the room,
the only sign – and it was huge –
was lettered, simply, DOG LICENSES.
A routine mix-up, doubtless,

as this must be as well: "First
time for both?" The reply – a check
in the box provided, size of a thumbtack,
on a page with room for

marriages of the future –
applied equally to the best and worst
of intentions. As he supplied their proof
of blood, of residence, of birth,

she held her pen above
a line marked "Married Name": for who
she was, and what of She was He,
was not to be resolved

by closing time. Meanwhile, her
first footprint for signature,
no bigger than a cat's paw, he
paused to get the gist of. She

who on all his life to come
had laid a claim – staggering
in its singleness
of purpose – had once

been living, evidently,
only for minutes … Asked now to raise
right hands, to swear they knew
of no impediment,

he set down his tennis racket;
their eyes, for an instant long
to be remembered, gravely met
in the sweet embrace of fear.

# Expectancy

*Japan Baptist Hospital, Kyoto*

One by one, we shuffle in
and take a quiet seat beneath
admonitory posters. Here's
Mrs. Shimoda, who, to judge from
her pink, quilted jumper appliquéd
with rabbits, and a fuzzy, enormous purse
emblazoned with cartoon characters,

appears to be in some confusion
as to whether she's going to have a baby
or (a greater miracle) become one;
and here's sorrowful Mrs. Fukumoto,
who hasn't looked well in weeks. Of course
I'm guessing – I'm a newcomer here,
and as the nurse calls out each name

just a touch louder than necessary
in a kindly, patronizing singsong,
I flinch. Thermometer under tongue,
blood pressure measured, I can clearly see
a needle creeping on the hateful scale
where serene Mrs. Oh, five months along,
checks in at less than I at two.

Yet don't I, in fact, want to feel the weight
of waiting once again? the way
(years ago) each birthday took years to arrive …
Oh to be sixteen at last, to drive,
to come home past eleven! To loosen
the hold of parents who'd grown to fear
time as a thing they only got less of,
while you knew, yourself, it was stored within.

Too early, I know, I begin to imagine
how the baby turns in its own waiting room,
as restlessly as I now turn
a health-book page in a half-learned language:
*Let's guard against* (illegible);
*be sure to* (illegible) *every day!*

But here's the man who can read it all:
the doctor – handsome, young, a bit proud,
as if the father of all our children –
billows in on a white, open-coated sail
and, bowing to us with nautical
briskness, takes the time to wish
the mates a benevolent good morning.

We murmur in kind; then, in a hush,
some dozen heads in unison
swivel to follow his form until
it vanishes behind a door.
Daily, I think, women just like us
are found normal there. Who shall be the first?
It's Mrs. Hino – although the nurse

has to call her twice, across the length
of eight abstracted months. She rises
slowly, resting, in a universal
gesture I've only begun to read,
one hand on the swell below her breasts
as though what's borne within
were here, and could be taken in her arms.

# Japanese Characters

1.

To look into a word as through a window
and address the thing itself: a simple wish,
and one calling me to a simpler time –
yet when can that have been? Life before English?
Conversant in the automatic doors
of an alphabet we barely need to press
for meaning sprung wide-open, now it seems
that again to sound things out and memorize
new, ramifying claims upon the eyes
is, piece by piece, to reconstruct a cosmos
I'd grown to think long set and spoken for.
Just as all life appears to have begun
the moment we were born, so around the sun
of native language orbit distant bodies
in atmospheres indigenously vague:
seen as through clouds, that's Venus thickly wrapped
in idioms colorful and yet inapt,
and Saturn's ring spins far too fast to wear.

The untold ideographs of Japanese
were Chinese first. To them are grafted two
syllabaries, native and phonetic,
which cling to borrowed roots. It grows aesthetic
to gaze upon these fruitless branchings, gnarled
so intricately no one in the world
can paint them right except a Japanese.
– Or so they'd have you think. Riding the bus,
my breath fogged on the pane, I puzzled out
streets whose billboards lettered in a scrawl
news that the world had slipped out of control.
Like insects some mad scientist had bred
to overrun an old, bad movie made
here in Japan, these characters were bound
to do us in … Enchanted, terrified,

at first I'd spend whole days cooped up behind
my room's milk-tinted glass. So little choice –
to view the brighter goings-on below
only by sliding free long streets of noise,
or to muffle them, but dim the light at once.

To look into a word as through a window
entirely clear – I'd given up that chance;
filmed over with the past, our TV screen
gave out on movies we'd already seen
at home. They'd been dubbed in Japanese,
but stubbornly, I felt as though I could
stare down the actors, coax them to unearth
my language lurking voiceless underneath.
Even at theaters, where we could hear
English so sharp we hung upon its edge,
characters white on black, and black on white
("subtitles" to the side, as hieroglyphic
as the crabbed marginalia on a page)
transported us to an unfeatured age
– past or future? it was hard to say – where night
is never clear enough to chart the stars.


2.

It's typhoon season. Above, a paper-thin
sky fills with figured clouds: an inky wash
the wind reconsiders swiftly with its brush.
Below, low-lying thunderheads (a queue
of black-haired students decked in navy blue,
each topped – like a dream of sun – with a yellow hat)
now and again burst out in laughter. Yet
they keep their civic files and parallels
that (paradoxically) might better suit
the strict march of our destined-to-repeat,

typecast, upstanding roman ABC's
whose measured zones our children (in their note-
books ruled like music staves) can fill
with nothing but the obsessive English trill.
How is it that the straitened Japanese,
living by Muzak and the megaphone,
tossed from such boats of reference stay afloat
with strokes on their letters fluent as a stream,
always familiar, never quite the same?
A mystery even when, some damp weeks later,
these start to take on clues of ... character.

Each I could set apart from all the rest
began to stalk me – as, once, a night of cards
turned every dream to numerals for words,
and every one called out to be the last:
after I'd run through King and Jack and Queen,
thousands of faces beckoned me for names,
thousands of names for faces yet unseen.
Old women, bent at pained diagonals
like orchid grass; others in Western chairs
asquat on pliant feet, so that four legs
of wood then stood in place of two of theirs –
stamped on my brain as whole and legible
at last, they seemed to press a further claim
on life's behalf: *you're here to crack the code.*
In whiteface, wig, kimono, here's a Bride.
The Guests need not be guessed: identified
as men in black suits, ties of white brocade,
women in black kimono with a hem
brushed with bamboo or crane. They carry gifts
the right size for *furoshiki,* a square
of wrapping cloth that's often lavender.
*Let there be no mistaking what we are,*

they seem to say, *it's chaos otherwise;*
*we'll limit human types to memorize.*


3.

One day in the paper, there's a story
on an amateur astronomer – a factory
worker who, gazing on the stars
just before dawn with plain binoculars
("a part of my routine patrol," he said),
spotted a nova no one else had found.
"I know the sky quite well, but this was luck,"
he told reporters, "to catch it at its peak" –
three minutes of intensity before
a star we wake to think the only one
blotted with light all light except its own.

"I know the sky quite well" – a vivid claim
suggesting a nightly rummage through its shelves
of scorpions and saucepans. We ourselves
can't hope to re-arrange the stars, but name
and name again, as if to cut to size
chaos that takes us hugely by surprise.
Like stars, like snow … when clusters of words come,
some melt, a disappointment, on the tongue,
their mystery gone – and yet their calligraphic
descent to comprehension followed traffic
down streets untraceable on any map.
And in sculptured garden-ponds, I now expect
bridges of stepstones one line can't connect,
grammar reversing like a velvet nap
whose shade of meaning fades upon my touch …
Gravity's upended. The universe

observes, it seems, the old misspeller's curse:
You have to have things down to look them up.

What am I learning, then? Perhaps to wish
less fervently the Romans will march in
dispensing justice: for every man one vote,
for every voice a single character.
(What should we call the lanes between the stars,
or the silence burning even at the cores
of those so bright they make us feverish?)
Just as new words, once never seen, appear
on every page as soon as known, the sky
prints images upon the clouded eye:
*distinguish these, and others will come clear.*
Immersed in truths by half, the vertigo
of apprehending patterns through a window
rinsed clean – until it may well not be there –
one questions further. "What's next to the Bear?"

# Welcome to Hiroshima

is what you first see, stepping off the train:
a billboard brought to you in living English
by Toshiba Electric. While a channel
silent in the TV of the brain

projects those flickering re-runs of a cloud
that brims its risen columnful like beer
and, spilling over, hangs its foamy head,
you feel a thirst for history: what year

it started to be safe to breathe the air,
and when to drink the blood and scum afloat
on the Ohta River. But no, the water's clear,
they pour it for your morning cup of tea

in one of the countless sunny coffee shops
whose plastic dioramas advertise
mutations of cuisine behind the glass:
a pancake sandwich; a pizza someone tops

with a maraschino cherry. Passing by
the Peace Park's floral hypocenter (where
how bravely, or with what mistaken cheer,
humanity erased its own erasure),

you enter the memorial museum
and through more glass are served, as on a dish
of blistered grass, three mannequins. Like gloves
a mother clips to coatsleeves, strings of flesh

hang from their fingertips; or as if tied
to recall a duty for us, *Reverence*
*the dead whose mourners too shall soon be dead,*
but all commemoration's swallowed up

in questions of bad taste, how re-created
horror mocks the grim original,
and thinking at last *They should have left it all*
you stop. This is the wristwatch of a child.

Jammed on the moment's impact, resolute
to communicate some message, although mute,
it gestures with its hands at eight-fifteen
and eight-fifteen and eight-fifteen again

while tables of statistics on the wall
update the news by calling on a roll
of tape, death gummed on death, and in the case
adjacent, an exhibit under glass

is glass itself: a shard the bomb slammed in
a woman's arm at eight-fifteen, but some
three decades on – as if to make it plain
hope's only as renewable as pain,

and as if all the unsung
debasements of the past may one day come
rising to the surface once again –
worked its filthy way out like a tongue.

# Henry Purcell in Japan

Here death does not confine itself
to the shuttered funeral parlor,
but roams from house to house like a beggar,
as quotidian as rain.
Today, once again, I saw them queuing
(the tail-coated men, black birds on a line,
the women columnar in kimono)
at a door where death had visited.
High bamboo placards draped in white
but muddied with sweeping characters
(names, perhaps, of those left behind)
were propped against the tiny house
like rafts secured to a bank.
Yet no one was going anywhere,

not the men whose task was to register
at felt-covered tables, brilliant red,
whatever was to be registered,
nor the women who made themselves at home
serving cups of pale green tea.
As I walked by they stared at me –
not angry, not stirring or saying a word,
but as if they expected me to concede
I didn't belong there. I remembered how,
standing in a Buddhist graveyard
some months ago – overseen by a crow
enormously foreign, and called *karasu* –
I'd known I was a trespasser.

It was their names that told me:
names recalled with unspeakable grace,
the chiseled letters liquid in stone
as if by brushwork. Reading down,
I felt as though the ashes of someone
whose name ran vertically might lie

differently, somehow, in the earth.
Such a small note seemed everything –
as today, once home from the funeral,
I listened to a choir sing Henry Purcell.
*Rejoice in the Lord alway,*
they sang; *And again I say rejoice!*
How explain to anyone the joy
of that single missing "s" – a winding path

down into a heritage so deep,
so long a part of me it seems
the very state of God?
The mellow, antiquated light
of drafty English chapels, and the comfort
of harmonies layered against the cold –
how exchange this god, like money,
for whatever imbues a Shinto shrine
painted the orange and gold of fire
with a bell-rung spirit more austere?
No, surely they were right,
the mourners who stared at me today;
schooled in other mysteries,
I stood as far from them

(or so it felt) as we all stood
from the foreign country of the dead.
Yet at home in my random corner
on truth, with no choice but to play
the world sung in a transposed key,
mine was another mourner's voice:
*And again I say rejoice.*

*from*

# Unfinished Painting

(1989)

# The Rebirth of Venus

He's knelt to fish her face up from the sidewalk
all morning, and at last some shoppers gather
to see it drawn – wide-eyed, and dry as chalk –
whole from the sea of dreams. It's she. None other

than the other one who's copied in the book
he copies from, that woman men divined
ages before a painter let them look
into the eyes their eyes had had in mind.

Love's called him too, today, though she has taught
him in her beauty to love best
the one who first had formed her from a thought.
One square of pavement, like a headstone (lest

anyone mistake where credit lies),
reads BOTTICELLI, but the long-closed dates
suggest, instead, a view of centuries
coming unbracketed, as if the gates

might swing wide to admit, here, in the sun,
one humble man into the pantheon
older and more exalted than her own.
    Slow gods of Art, late into afternoon

let there be light: a few of us drop the wish
into his glinting coinbox like a well,
remembering the forecast. Yet he won't rush
her finish, though it means she'll have no shell

to harbor in; it's clear enough the rain
will swamp her like a tide, and lion-hearted
he'll set off, black umbrella sprung again,
envisioning faces where the streets have parted.

# Reading Room

*Williston Memorial Library, Mount Holyoke College*

The chapter ends. And when I look up
from a sunken pose in an easy chair
(half, or more than half, asleep?)
the height and heft of the room come back;
darkly, the pitched ceiling falls
forward like a book.
Even those mock-Tudor stripes
have come to seem like unread lines.
Oh, what I haven't read!

– and how the room, importunate
as a church, leans as if reading *me:*
the three high windows in the shape
of a bishop's cap, and twenty girls
jutting from the walls like gargoyles
or (more kindly) guardian angels
that peer over the shoulder, straight
into the heart. Wooden girls who exist
only above the waist –

whose wings fuse thickly into poles
behind them – they hold against their breasts,
alternately, books or scrolls
turned outward, as if they mean to ask:
*Have you done your Rhetoric today?*
*Your passage of Scripture? Your Natural*
*Philosophy?* In their arch, archaic
silence, one can't help but hear a
mandate from another era,

and all too easy to discount
for sounding quaint. Poor
Emily Dickinson, when she was here,
had to report on the progress of
her soul toward Christ. (She said: *No hope.*)

Just as well no one demands
to know *that* anymore … Yet
one attends, as to a lecture,
to this stern-faced architecture –

Duty is Truth, Truth Duty – as one
doesn't to the whitewashed, low
ceilings of our own. Despite
the air these angels have of being
knowing (which mainly comes by virtue
of there being less to know back then),
there's modesty in how they flank
the room like twenty figureheads;
they won't, or can't, reveal who leads

the ship you need to board. Beneath
lamps dangled from the angels' hands –
stars to steer us who knows where –
thousands of periodicals
unfurl their thin, long-winded sails;
back there, in the unlovely stacks,
the books sleep cramped as sailors.
So little time to learn what's worth
our time! No one to climb that stair

and stop there, on the balcony
walled like a pulpit or a king's
outlook in a fairy tale,
to set three tasks, to pledge rewards.
Even the angels, after all,
whose burning lamps invoke a quest
further into the future, drive
us back to assimilate the past
before we lose the words.

No, nobody in the pulpit
but for the built-in, oaken face
of a timepiece that – I check my watch –
still works. As roundly useful as
the four-armed ceiling fans that keep
even the air in circulation,
it plays by turns with hope and doubt;
hard not to read here, in the clock's
crossed hands, the paradox

of Time that is forever running out.

# The Annunciation

Unparalleled on Earth, their faces look
alike – like open pages from the Book
wherein their story's told and was foretold,
since prophecies are made to be recalled;
like Gabriel's wings, one iridescent, one
behind illumined purely by assumption.
He, gazing in her eyes, taught all that he

could teach her of divine tautology
the moment when his profile met the plane
her profile had established first as human.
They do it all with mirrors: odd to conceive
her image in our other mother, Eve,
and yet what's odd must, doubled, come out even –
like unlikely Eden, verified by Heaven.

# A Case of Netsuke

Wise, size of a peachpit, nut-
brown, wizened, intricate,
    the Badger Dressed in Lotus Leaf
stands tall in his sheet: as grand
or grander than Rodin's Balzac, and

even smacks of evil, as
he has the full, unruffled gaze
    of the Wolf under Grandmother's nightgown.
*The better to draw you close, my dear,*
to a museum-case of obscure

Japanese bibelots. Each
a tangible anecdote, they reach
    first to us from English tags:
Starving Dog, Herdboy with Flute,
Dutchman with Moneybag, or Stoat

on Pumpkin, Bean Pods, Pile of Fish …
As if that wordless, brimming wish
    to get everything said before
we're dead might be fulfilled at last,
they speak to us of a lost

life we may have lived once, though
it's daunting we should think so –
    for what could we have had in common
with Seated Demon or Drunken Sprite?
And by what twist does Thwarted Rat-

Catcher call up the aim of Art?
Yet that look of his, of being thwarted,
    as he crouches over the empty cage
and, too late, lifts his club to thwack
the rat scaling his own back,

is intimately familiar – like
the downturned, howling mask of tragic
    theater. If somehow the play
of his features also shows he's half-
laughing, it may be at himself:

grinning, with a shrunken skull's
grim triumph, or like a set of false
    teeth that's doubled over in
age-yellowed ivory,
he's detached from his unsavory

and blunt stabs at success. The gift,
he chides himself, is to be swift
    and tireless; to hit on a connection –
not just pummel the rat but tell
the whole tale in a nutshell.

# Unfinished Painting

Dark son, whose face once shone like this,
oiled from well within the skin
of canvas, and whose liquid eyes
were brown as rootbeer underneath
    a crewcut's crown, just washed,

his body's gone unfinished now
more than thirty years – blank tent
of bathrobe like a choirboy's surplice
over the cassock's stroke of color,
    a red pajama collar.

Drawn as if it might reveal
the dotted hills of Rome, a drape
behind him opens on a wall
she'd painted with a roller once.
    Everything made at home –

she made the drapes, she made the boy,
and then, pure joy, remade him in
a pose to bear his mother's hope:
the deep, three-quarter gaze; the tome
    he fingers like a pope.

Is this the History of Art
he marks her place in, or – wait –
that illustrated Brothers Grimm
she'd inscribed for him, his name enclosed
    within it like a heart?

Hard to sort out … She rarely put
the final touch on anything
when he was young. It seems that bringing
the real boy up had taken time
    away from painting him

(no crime); she'd also failed to think
of him – back then her only child –
as truly done, and one child only,
but marvelled as he altered like
    the light she painted by.

… Like, too, the image he's retained
of the sun in her, now set,
her eyes that took him back, and in,
squinting as he squirmed, appraising,
    praising him again,

so that, when sifting through her basement
stacked with a dozen such false starts,
and lifting this one, lighter than
he thought it ought to be, to frame
    and hang in his apartment,

he saw in his flushed face how she'd
re-created there what rose
and fell in hers: the confidence
she forfeited each time she dared
    think of an audience.

*Who* (she must have asked) *would care?*
He does: that finished head conveys
still to him how, sought in a crowd,
a loved one stands apart – he's taller,
    comes in a different shade.

# Elegies for Etsuko

1.

Begin with the last and unrecorded scene –
how rashly, with a length of rope,
she'd gathered up an end to hope?
Or unravel these six years
to where my life first tangled up with hers?
Or, midway, to that greater knot: again

the line of thought loops back, heart-
broken, to where she reckoned life to start.
Her wedding day. The Bride.
And in truth, that day I shed
a veil of happy tears: to see that snow
mountain of kimono

and, falling from the pinnacle
of her lacquered wig, the fog of silk
over a face too shy, too proud
to lift. Who'd made her up? – the natural
milk of her skin absorbed in chalk,
a slope of powder

down to her collar, pulled low at the back.
Viewed from behind, a woman's neck
is (say the Japanese – and so she'd say)
her most erotic feature.
But I think she was that day
a hybrid sort of fantasy, a creature

sparked by a wand, then shrinking like that star
when the TV goes black. Am I unkind?
Darling, we guess at how you came unwound;
at how many times you drunkenly replayed
that trade of sacred *sake* and were made
Queen for a Day again on the VCR.

2.

Given how brief a spell
happiness usually is, and the ways
people are forever failing us,
with time it shocks me less you didn't mind
leaving the two of them behind;
yes yes, I see that, I see it very well …
But do you mean to say you were willing
never again to wear a new dress?
And never again to choose one for your daughter?
Long before she was born, or mine was,
we'd go on window-shopping sprees
in children's stores. Saccharine, but true.
*I can't stand it,* one of us would say; *can you?*
 – A bonnet or a tasseled sock would send
us off: half-stifled, giggling cries …

In the end, you didn't think to find
even a rag to shield her eyes.
Because you had gone blind.


3.

In Keiko's brain these words are Japanese
in bits and pieces     none of them is written
nobody's here to hear the words she knows
nobody's here     just Mother on the ceiling
her face is closed her face     long face her hair
not crying now     she tries *okaasan*     Mother
the word that calls up everything
and nothing moves at all     oh there's her ball

4.

Ages between the day I left Japan
and the first time I saw you again: the last
time, too. New Year's Eve in Rome.
Foreigners both, we soon pick up that wordless, winking giddiness we'd had: as light
a burden as our daughters, whom we lift
to watch the soaring fireworks. Each time the sky
blows up again, and then begins to cry
in sputters – whistling, molten streaks of tears –
we laugh: *See? Nothing to be afraid of …*
And in the window, too, we see ourselves
reflected kindly in our girls: *They'll learn
to be mothers just like us.* How long since you
were known as Hara-san (Miss Hara)! These days
it haunts me, that when you married you erased
your first name too – and as an honor asked
I call you by a childhood nickname, Ekko.
Ekko. Echo. *Ecco:* the champagne
cork pops, the skies explode, repeat
that automatic gunfire to the heart:
Ekko, who would not toast the year again.


5.

These vacant months I've tried to disavow
that something's happened to you, something dire.
I know you're gone for good. And this is how

I've figured out you've made your final bow
(at last, the proof 's so small that we require!) –
were you alive, you would have called by now.

More clues come than I'd willingly allow:
if they hadn't shoveled you into the fire
(I know you're gone for good, and this is how)

and buried you beneath a maple bough,
you would have dropped a line or sent a wire.
Were you alive, you would have called by now.

The phone's the lifeline of the lost *hausfrau*.
But now what's at your ear? The angel's lyre?
I know you're gone for good, and this is how

I turn the same line over like a plow,
since there is nothing further to inquire.
Were you alive, you would have called by now

to greet me in your faulty English grammar.
Your silence shows precisely how you are.
I know you're gone for good. And this is how:
were you alive, you would have called by now.


6.

Up here's where you end up. Room with a view
in (of all places) Edinburgh, though who's
willing to predict she'll feel at home
with dying anywhere? Why not the random
furnished flat in Scotland? What we own,
what we are owned by, are no less transient
than other plots of earth we briefly rent ...

Parking across the street, we stay inside
as if we hope (we fear) you're still up there
in a state of mind precarious but alive:
you mustn't be allowed to think we're spying.

You seem to know I knew I'd have to come;
that your husband's brought me here, a half-year later.
Oh, anything we do may set the chain

reaction going once more in that brown
study of your brain; we'd have to live
through losing you again; we'd have to choose …
Why is it your apartment's set ablaze
and no one else's? Why is it in the pitch
of six o'clock in winter, nothing's on
in all the building – just the silhouette

of a woman coming slowly to your window
to watch the Christmas lights down Princes Street
illuminate toy people and their things?
… Unless, somehow, you're giving us the ghost
of a chance to guess how singularly bright
you'd felt yourself to burn, engulfed in flame
none of us ever saw, much less put out?


7.

Once, in Kyoto, we gossipped past the temple
graveyard where you'd lie, on to the shrine

where you wanted us to buy two paper dolls:
featureless, pure white, the kind a child

cuts in hand-holding chains across a fold.
An old priest had us sign them both for luck.

I wrote across the heart, you down the spine,
then quaintly (so I thought) you drew two smiles …

That was before you snapped your pretty neck.
Happy you may have been, but never simple.


    8.

Happy you may have been …
There were whole years when I'd have said
you were happier than anyone.
You've now been dead

(and been enclosed
in the double mystery of what
that is, and why you thought
it might be best)

for long enough it's time
to more than forgive the sin
of express despair, the crime
of not being what we seem,

or of not being anything
in particular … for isn't that
really what you feared you were?
Sometimes the note

you didn't write (because
you needed all the energy you had
to do the deed? because
there's no cause in the mad,

for whom the world's a small
footstool kicked aside?)
looms real and legible.
It says you died

because you'd come to think that love
is not enough. Well, I'd
probably have agreed,
advised you to find work, to read.

And now love's pain, your curse,
is all I have. Forgive me ... What worse
punishment for suicide
than having died?


9.
On the master list we keep
imagining the scribes still keep
religiously, up there in space,
of every human life, let
them not neglect to fill the line
for Etsuko Akai, who's gone
from Earth at twenty-eight.

In the impossible blue dark,
let all the bearded saints and rain-
bowed angels sorrow can invent
take her, who never made her mark,
and gladly mark the day for love
not of what she might have been,
but what she humbly was.

For surely they have reams of time
to celebrate the perfect moon
set in her attentive face,
where pallidly, one shallow crater –
a pockmark time could not efface –
glossed the ancient and unwritten
flaws of her Creator.

Since they will all be there for ages,
let them in their inventory
preserve in lucent, gilt-edged pages
those things I would myself record:
such as the way she'd tell a story –
she'd race, and trip, and laugh so hard
we'd ask her to start over.

# The Moon and Big Ben

STOP. Here, in our widened eyes,
they're nearly of a size.
And loom so close they seem to miss
    meeting by a nose,

the two moons of a pair of glasses
slowly disengaging as
the left one rises up to peer
    over the other's shoulder.

She finds there, in the Gothic news-
print of his measured face,
a daily mirror of the Times –
    the catalogue of crimes

and speeches, elections, electrocutions,
the columns and the revolutions
bringing new tyrannies to power
    almost by the hour –

and sees he stands for the imperial
notion of direction. The serial,
progressive sequence of events
    has, he booms, consequence.

Well. It is an ancient dial-
ectic, and it may take her awhile
(or forever) who whispers in his ear
    the limits of the linear

repeatedly, and every night,
to prove she has it right;
but there can be no gainsaying how,
    floating higher, smaller now

(and soon in ever-slimmer crescents),
she's not yet lost her essence.

# Doubles

Months later, when she's begun to breathe
more easily without him, she exhumes
    a roll of film, like a mummy, from
the camera's black chamber. Her memory
    of everything, not only him,

has gone a little fuzzy – that's
a price she's had to pay – and in a rush
    she drops it off at the shop like sheets
she hasn't time to launder. It's all the same
    in the chemical bath, the surfacing frame

after frame of grandchild, sunrise, garden –
and all the same to the man who hands them back
    to her, thick and bland as a deck
of never-shuffled cards. Yet when she deals
    them out on that snowbound night, she finds –

somewhat to her surprise – the days
(each fenced in commemorative white border)
    again at her fingertips, and in order:
leafing from winter into fall, and fall
    into summer, a movie run in reverse,

she's happy. And then she slows like a hearse.
It's him. Oh God, it's him. She thought she'd given
    all of him away – his ties
to the boys, his hundred handkerchiefs, his shoes –
    but here he is. There's more of him to lose.

Receive it like his posthumous postcard – a "wish
I were here"? How long did this message, curled as if
    in a bottle, wait to bring its proof
of some blue passage home from another world?
    *Who* took this last, lost picture? She can't

remember. Rooted here in her boots,
she knows it can't have been herself: she's *there,*
     in her tennis dress and fresh-permed hair;
she's living next to his seersucker shorts, the blinding
     glint on his glasses, the shine on his balding head,

     she's standing with him behind the net
and squinting into an unseen sun – or, now,
     into the mirror of her own
face that has grown used to one alone.
     Dear man. If she could kiss that hand –

     the hand he's flung across her shoulder,
warm from the game ... But she understands no feat
     of athletic prowess will ever let
her jump that sagging net, and the game's unfair:
     the two of them against the one of her.

# Summer 1983

None of us remembers these, the days
when passing strangers adored us at first sight,
just for living, or for strolling down the street;
praised all our given names; begged us to smile …
you, too, in a little while,
my darling, will have lost all this,
asked for a kiss will give one, and learn
how love dooms us to earn
love once we can speak of it.

# Dead Letters

### 1.

*Dear Mrs. Salter: Congratulations! You*
(no need to read on – yet I always do)
*may have won the sweepstakes, if you'll send …*
Is this how it must end?
Or will it ever end? The bills, all paid,
come monthly anyway, to cheer the dead.
*BALANCE:* decimal point and double o's
like pennies no one placed upon your eyes.
I never saw you dead – you simply vanished,
your body gone to Science, as you wished:
I was the one to send you there, by phone,
on that stunned morning answering the blunt
young nurse who called, wanting to "clear the room."
"Take her," I said, "I won't be coming in" –
couldn't bear to see your cherished face with more
death in it than was there five days before.
But now, where are you really? From the mail
today, it seems, you might almost be well:
*Dear Patient: It's been three years since your eyes*
*were checked …* A host of worthy causes vies
for your attention: endangered wildlife funds,
orphans with empty bowls in outstretched hands,
political prisoners, Congressmen. The *LAST*
*ISSUE*s of magazines are never last.
And now you've shored up on some realtors' list,
since word went out you've "moved" to my address:
*Dear New Apartment Owner: If you rent …*
Mother, in daydreams sometimes I am sent
to follow you, my own forwarding text
*Dear Mrs. Salter's Daughter: You are next.*

2.

When I try to concentrate
on who you were,
images of you blur
and pulsate, like the clothes
left in your closet –

every size from four to fourteen,
not progressively,
but back and forth again:
testaments to Treatment
after Treatment.

Injected, radiated,
bloated, balded, nauseated;
years in an iron wig that ill
fit or befitted you;
then more years, unexpected,

of a cobweb gray you grew
in thanks to covet:
lurching from reprieve to reprieve,
you taught yourself to live
with less and less,

and so did we –
even, at last, without the giddy
vastness of your love,
so painfully withdrawn when pain
became all you could think of.

Trying not to feel
that nothing, not even love
or death, is original,
like other mourners I've
turned up happy photographs –

of the ruby-lipsticked girl
(in black-and-white, but I can tell)
on your wedding day; or, here, a scene
in a hallway I'd hardly know was ours
but for that gilt barometer.

Had I lost that about you?
Your regal touch – china in green
and gold; silk Oriental dresses?
… Days that made you queen
of nothing but your high-backed bed

convinced you
you'd been singled out to die.
Yet here you are,
a smiling hostess at the door
bidding your friends goodbye:

What blessedness!
– To think that once
you hadn't had to be the focus,
could go on living unpitied,
even unnoticed.

3.

Dinner in Boston. I am twenty-three,
and you have come to see
your grown-up daughter in her element.
My choice is cheap and almost elegant:
crêpes and spinach salad, a carafe
of chilled house wine we laugh

companionably over. Memory drifts
back to well-set tables shared at home –
those animated dinners you would chair
(the Salter Seminars, my boyfriend called them)
where you taught me to admire
the complex givens of your gifts

for life. Accomplished cook,
stickler for decorum, you liked to shock
us with the heedless, vocal sweep
of your opinions: on the Catholic Church
(you hate it, so you think – hate it so much
you'll find a slow way back);

the saintliness of Adlai; Armageddon.
(Once, you greeted me from school with news
the Chinese had invaded us: a thrill
that never found its way to print,
but you shrugged off my complaint:
"If they haven't done it yet, you know they will.")

Tonight, Newbury Street –
scene of my happy lunch hours, of the young
executives with ice cream cones
dripping down their hands, bright students in new jeans –
outside our window takes, as night sifts down,
that memorializing cast of light

you seem to shed on things, all by yourself.
Even when all is well (the illness
more under control than less,
you're devoting all your time to sculpture
bigger than you are – filling every shelf
in the garage!) I still recapture

moments before they're over.
*She loved me so, that when I praised her shirt
she took it off her back,* or
*We drank four cups of tea apiece* … Alert
always to what perishes, I invert
your low, confiding chuckle now and pour

its darkness like a stain across our table.
"Can you remember Grandma's laugh? I can't,"
I interrupt, and having voiced the fear,
immediately am able:
it sounded like a baby's xylophone,
thrown down a flight of stairs.

Who could have forgotten *that*?
I laugh myself – but now I've spoiled
the mood, or turned it oversweet,
and you reach into your magic purse
for a snapshot of your mother. "Here, it's yours."
Stunned how soon my eyes have filled

with tears – how easy it has been
to give a pleasing answer –
you seem relieved to put to death
a momentary fright not only mine.
Now, your own forever-
unrecorded voice cut short by cancer,

I still find myself asking: dear
as she was, didn't you know
it's you I was crying for?


4.

We're on our way to the hospital
for the twenty-thousandth time.
You used to drive – then I;
lately, we've piled into a taxi.
Each week a new man takes the rap
for bumps and jolts; if not for him
(you imply) we'd have a pleasant trip.
Shrunken and old, collapsible,
head in my lap, you start up in alarm:
"Mary Jo – I think I'm ill."

Forgive me that I laughed!
It's too late to apologize;
but that you could find it in you still
to register surprise –
that *you'd* hope to be well …
It kept you alive, of course,
those years of asking visitors
"Are your ears ringing?" as if there might
someday be found a blanket cause
for pains that kept you up all night.


5.

If you could see your daughter, no green thumb,
tending the philodendron
you sent me when my baby girl was born!
If you could see my daughter: that refrain

twists like a crimping weed, a vine of pain
around the joy of everything she learns.

And yet it intertwines
forever, I perceive, your life and mine.
From time to time, a heart-shaped leaf will turn
yellow and fall – in falling a leaf torn
out of your life again,
the story I must constantly revive.

I water it and live;
water and wait for other plants to bloom.
I took them from your room
nearly a year ago now, poinsettias
of that wizened, stricken Christmas
you floated through five days before the end.

One's inky-red; the other paper-white …
You too were one to note
life's artful correspondences.
But I can't let them go,
not yet; and granted time to tend
a growing tenderness, I send

more letters, Mother – these despite
the answers you can't write.

*from*

# Sunday Skaters

(1994)

# Boulevard du Montparnasse

Once, in a doorway in Paris, I saw
the most beautiful couple in the world.
They were each the single most beautiful thing in the world.
She would have been sixteen, perhaps; he twenty.
Their skin was the same shade of black: like a shiny Steinway.
And they stood there like the four-legged instrument
of a passion so grand one could barely imagine them
ever working, or eating, or reading a magazine.
Even they could hardly believe it.
Her hands gripped his belt loops, as they found each other's eyes,
because beauty like this must be held onto,
could easily run away on the power
of his long, lean thighs; or the tiny feet of her laughter.
I thought: now I will write a poem,
set in a doorway on the Boulevard du Montparnasse,
in which the brutishness of time
rates only a mention; I will say simply
that if either one should ever love another,
a greater beauty shall not be the cause.

# Young Girl Peeling Apples

*(Nicolaes Maes)*

It's all
an elaborate pun:
the red peel of ribbon
twisted tightly about the bun
at the crown of her apple-

round head;
the ribbon coming loose in the real
apple-peel she allows to dangle
from her lifted hand; the table
on which a basket of red

apples
waits to be turned into more
white-fleshed apples in a water-
filled pail on the floor;
her apron that fills and falls

empty,
a lapful of apples piling on
like the apron itself, the napkin,
the hems of her skirts – each a skin
layered over her heart, just as he

who has
painted her at her knife
paints the brush that puts life
in her, apple of his eye: if
there's anything on earth but this

unbroken
concentration, this spiral
of making while unmaking while
the world goes round, neither the girl
nor he has yet looked up, or spoken.

# The Twelfth Year

That autumn we walked and walked around the lake
as if around a clock whose hands swept time
and again back to the hour we'd started from,
that high noon in midsummer years before
when I in white had marched straight to my place
beside you and was married and your face
held in it all the hours I hoped to live.
Now, as we talked in circles, grim, accusing,
we watched the green trees turning too and losing
one by one every leaf, those bleeding hearts.
And when they all had fallen, to be trod
and crumbled underfoot, when flaming red
had dulled again to dun, to ash, to air,
when we had seen the other's hurts perfected
and magnified like barren boughs reflected
upside-down in water, then the clouds
massed overhead and muffled us in snow,
answered the rippling lake and stopped the O
of its nightmare scream. The pantomime
went on all winter, nights without a word
or thoughts to fit one, days when all we heard
was the ticking crunch of snowboots on the track
around the lake, the clock we thought we either
were winding up or running down or neither.
Spring came unexpected. We thought the cold
might last forever, or that despite the thaw
nothing would grow again from us; foresaw
no butter-yellow buds, no birds, no path
outward into a seasoned innocence.
When the circle broke at last it wasn't silence
or speech that helped us, neither faith nor will
nor anything that people do at all;
love made us green for no sure cause on earth
and grew, like our children, from a miracle.

# Moving

Like planning one's own funeral:
papers finally in their file,
change-of-address cards like a will

directing where everything should be going:
shut windows and the billowing
curtains that caught the breath of spring

folded like shrouds in the spiritless
coffins of labeled cardboard boxes;
boxes and boxes and more boxes

lined up on the lawn like gravestones,
then lifted groaningly into vans –
how could we bear to make such plans

if we didn't believe that purgatory
is waiting for us precisely where
our cartons will next see the air,

the sealed flaps opening like a pair
of French windows on another story?

# Poppies

### 1.

For years, above the white sofa, it hung
as a shimmering emblem of home –
the path white-hot, the blurred
strokes of the loaded brush Renoir meant
to convey summer's plenty and the rush
of the child who led the way.
They were going home

through a heedless field of green and yellow,
weeds tickling ankles, insects ticking –
a mass of happiness.
Just steps behind the child was a woman,
the pulsing heart of things, the red
parasol behind her head
a medal of motherhood, a halo,

and here and there, the red parasols
of poppies were twirling on their stems,
each held safely by the hand
of roots unseen in the soil.
There was so much you couldn't see.
No house beyond the gate on the right.
No face on the two black-clad

figures descending from the crest
of the hill. Grandparents, I decided.
That dot was her big black parasol.
No telling how long an inch
of canvas might take them, or if they'd catch
up ever. But the child had lost,
as it gained on them, nothing as yet.

2.

Staring into the postcard,
I follow the shrunken path
upward until the black
parasol, with a surreal
insouciance, leads me back

behind the hill, far back
to a television screen
where I saw this only once.
I would have been six or seven,
now old enough that a cold

meant no school, and I lay
in my parents' bed like a queen.
Mother was out in the garden,
my lunch was on the tray,
and a movie in black and white

flickered with nuances
I was happy not to get.
Then a door slammed. And the mother
in a long, old-fashioned dress
was rushing out the gate,

a mammoth black umbrella
above her averted face.
Thunder was splitting things,
and the violins explained
that this was really the end,

and the child cried at the window
filmed from the outside
so you couldn't hear the tears

running down with the rain.
I was locked in bed, and the movie

was taking the mother away,
and frame after frame was a door
shutting fast, and I had no key.
When the child knelt to peer
through a keyhole in the shape

of a teardrop, I understood
she was never coming home.
How long could the little scene
of abandonment have taken?
I turned it into a dream,

and played it over and over
until it became one seamless
parable that arched
from parasol to umbrella,
a place to search for cover

before I woke and found
the nightmare dried
to nothingness in the sun.
You – you've now been gone
ten years; been dead longer

than I'd lived when I learned
you'd leave forever.
Ten years ago, beneath
the shelter of some tree
or other, as you'd asked,

your child stood with an urn
of ashes, and scattered them
to the breeze, as if a random
handful might crop up
in the field as poppies.

# Lullaby for a Daughter

Someday, when the sands of time
invert, may you find perfect rest
as a newborn nurses from
the hourglass of your breast.

# Lament

Waking in her crib, the boat
they pushed her off in long ago,
although she stood to shake the rail
and wail at them,
                              she's all at sea.
Nothing familiar in the dark
until she rubs it from her eyes:
gray bear, gray ceiling where the moons
and stars turn, turn away.
                              Why
wouldn't she cry? For out there, perched
at table's edge, unreachable,
white to the brim, supremely real,
the bottle with the golden nipple
glows like a lighthouse.

# Icelandic Almanac

1. *The Sky in Akureyri*
in July is high and broad,
with here and there a scrap of cloud
stretched like a hat that doesn't fit.

Nothing can put a cap on it,
this light that lasts all night,
even when the long, elliptic sun,

a low plane circling for an open
runway, nearly lands –
but, throwing up its hands, ascends

by slow degrees again.
After a while, though every motion
tends to the horizontal, what

you're hoping for isn't sundown but
rainfall: something to precipitate
the end of a relentless,

restless Paradise.
Time an eternity of space ...
Time watching as dark, overblown

clouds hold their breath all day, then
drily fly away; time beaten thin
enough it may have passed

entirely into mist.
When at last the first
cloud dissolves, like a tablet

in its own water, it's also like a thought,
whose moving parts are discrete, caught
in the murky downpour of feeling.

But this is not the end. Trailing
behind with its blanket, failing
to see what can't be done, the sun

resumes that setting – or sitting – on
a fine, pink line it's drawn
to divide today from tomorrow.


2. *The Dark in Reykjavik*
    in December is far
    from monolithic – not
a block of static blackness, but
    an inky, effervescent

    potion ever
    carbonated by the dots
of thousands of electric lights.
    The stars are burning

    ceaselessly somewhere, and here
    you remember that: orderly
stacks of them, floor by floor.
    And neon at eleven in

    the morning makes
    everything you've done so far
(breakfast, getting dressed) appear
    precocious, blazoned triumph –

  trumpeted, as well, by twin
 high beams turning corners for
the dark at the end of their tunnels; or
   by inverted funnels thrown

  from a line of streetlamps.
 Not monolithic, no, and yet
come noon when, like the spangled velvet
   drape the poet speaks of, night

  parts (a space enough
 to poke your face through; a spotlit
hour or two a playwright might
   illuminate the limits of

  our life in), gratitude
 rises up. Even for that wall-to-wall
cloud rolled across the sky, as dull
   and sullen as a pearl,

  whose muffled glow
 forecasts another sort: not sun-
shine's diamond, and meant more to be seen
   than see by; obscurity

  dressed in white;
 sub-zero understudy flown in from
everywhere at once – in sum,
   snow filling in for light.

# Sunday Skaters

These days,
the sky composes promises
    and rips them to pieces. White
        as a sheet, this morning's cloud-
    cover crumples now and again, then snaps
back white when a gust shakes it out. Out
    for the usual stroll,

    I stop
to look at March in its muddles:
    in a snowbank (black
        boulders of old ice new-
    mottled with powder), puddles
that must be from yesterday's
    slanting rain and hail,

    which fell
as if from one combined
    salt-and-pepper shaker. I wind
        as the wind does, chased downhill,
    past the soaked, concrete blocks
of apartments and the dented heaps
    of corrugated-iron houses

    left out
in the rain for years and years,
    the olive-green of their raised
        surfaces sprayed with rust
    in vertical bands. Venetian blinds –
more metal, pulled to metal sills, but
    going against the grain –

      mix up
the texture, as does, still better, this
    one lace-curtained window fringed
       with icicles.
    Since they may melt in an hour,
on a day when everything's changed
    so often, one pauses for that pristine

      tension
of winter held in suspension. Just
    then, at the bottom of the street,
      I see the skaters:
    the luck of it
on a Sunday! The chances thin
    as the ice they coast on –

      to find
the snow wind-dusted off,
    and an hour both cold and warm enough
      overlapping leisure.
    From here, the disc of the pond
looks like one of those children's games
    designed for the palm,

      whose goal
is all at once to sink each silver
    ball into a hole.
      What each of them is slipping
    into, though, is another color:
approached, they glide by in mint and mauve
    and lilac, turquoise, rose, down

            parkas
in shiny nylon glimpsed
        for an instant. Like a clock
            with too many hands, gone haywire,
        the pond's a rink of hockey sticks: tock-
tick-tick as the puck
        takes a shortcut from four to six

            to nine.
Look at that girl in the long braid, trailed
        by her mother, a close-cropped beauty
            who takes on a heart-speeding
        force, as they spin hand-in-
hand, and a teenager's sheen;
        and catch that baby buggy,

            pushed off
freely as a swing down the ice …
        Stock still at the clock's center,
            the pin that everything hinges on:
        the wide, fur-circled face
of a small boy who feels his place
        in the larger frame.

            It's all
about time, about time! Above us,
        a frosty layer of cloud takes the weight
            of the sun's one warming foot,
        bright as a yellow boot. Although,
as yet, nothing flies but the snow's
        negative (flurries

*Sunday Skaters*

            of crows
appearing from nowhere), rather
    than wait for the other shoe
          to drop – that shower
    of rain, or sleet, or something, sure
to come – I rush into a coffee shop,
      and close the door.

            And close
my eyes, in time, when a cup
    of muddy, quivering liquid releases
          erasing clouds of steam, calling up
    in the sudden dark the skaters' dizzy
scissoring and see-sawing, scoring
      lines over, and over again.

# Frost at Midnight

*For I was reared*
*In the great city, pent 'mid cloisters dim,*
*And saw nought lovely but the sky and stars.*
*But thou, my babe! shalt wander like a breeze*
*By lakes and sandy shores ...*

– Coleridge

1.

His children tuckered out, tucked in (three girls
jammed in one bedroom, the boy in the only other),
and Elinor dozing where the dining room
would be if they'd had room, the "Yank from Yankville,"
as he liked to call himself, was wide awake.
It was midnight, on the fifteenth of September,
1912, and Frost was thirty-eight.
Tonight, he'd stay up late before the fire
in his Morris chair, as he often did, and write
to Susan Hayes Ward of *The Independent,*
who'd been the first to put his name in print.
Hard to believe that he, New Hampshire teacher
and half-hearted farmer, poet of little note,
just days before had boarded *The Parisian*
from Boston to Glasgow, then taken the train to London
with all of those now sleeping in his care.
Or that a tip from a retired policeman
(they knew no one in England, not a soul)
had led them to the village of Beaconsfield,
and a cottage called The Bungalow (or Bung Hole,
in the family lingo) for a monthly rent
of twenty dollars. Why were they here?

They'd flipped a coin.
Heads England, tails Vancouver – the nickel rose
silver like the moon from the Atlantic
they'd cross, sea-sick, to see it land again.
And now they lived behind a looming hedge

of American laurel, taller than any he
had seen at home. He wasn't here to pose
at Englishness, although the place was quaint,
all right: the muffin man had stepped
out of the nursery rhyme to walk their street
with the flypaper man; the knife-grinder; the man
who dangled pots and pans for sale from a wagon
drawn by a donkey. All this the children loved,·
and Elinor might still fulfill her dream
sometime of sleeping under thatch. But no,
he hadn't come to write about such things.
At the bottom of his trunk the manuscripts
of some hundred poems waited to be sorted
into two books or three, and he'd write more
about the world he knew and had left behind.

His firstborn Elliott dead (his fault, he thought –
he'd called for the wrong doctor); later a daughter,
her mother's namesake, who lived not quite two days –
he wouldn't stop to brood on those troubles now.
Tonight his mood was defiant, even "aberrant,"
he wrote to Susan Ward. He'd "achieve something
solid enough to sandbag editors with."
After all, it was just a few miles from here
that Milton, in a cottage like this (shared
with *his* three daughters) finished *Paradise Lost*. ·
And a mile or two the other way that Gray,
redeemed by glory, lay in a country churchyard.
"To London town what is it but a run?"
he closed in singsong, adding he'd step out
to the yard, before bed, to watch the city lights
in the distance "flaring like a dreary dawn."

Not quite – but a visionary flourish?
A biographer named Walsh, who went to live

in The Bungalow long after, noted how
London remains some twenty-one miles off.
Equipped with a naked eye, then, Frost could never
have caught the faintest glimmer of the city.
But was this the night the first biographer
would write of as the turning point? The night
the poems were taken from the trunk and sorted
into the first of all the selves he left?
It was sometime in September or October.
Frost sat on the cold floor. From time to time,
he'd crumple a ball and toss it in the fire.
He saw, in the hearth, the lights of London blaze
each time he found a poem to sacrifice:
that way the ones he saved could shine the brighter.
Or it may be, as the curling pages turned
brilliant a fierce instant, then to ash,
he was thinking of the sallow leaves that fell
indifferently outside, beyond the laurel,
and was terrified of their unwritten message.
By October's end, the book was done and out,
typed by his eldest, Lesley; a Mrs. Nutt
(who shrugged "the day of poetry is past")
allowed she was nonetheless "disposed" to publish.
*A Boy's Will.* He'd left boyhood after all.


2.

As a boy might skip a stone across a pond,
skim over fifty-one Octobers, to
the President with the winning smile. He'll fall
in less than one month's time in the Dallas sun.
He comes to return the favor of a white-
maned legend, lionized past recognition.
Once, squinting in the glare, fumbling with pages
that seemed on fire, the poet had declaimed

by heart (though he misspoke the young man's name)
a poem to inaugurate The New Frontier.
Robert Frost is dead; a library in his honor
at Amherst College today is dedicated.
"He knew the midnight as well as the high noon,"
Kennedy says. And now the library shelves
behind him will begin to accrete their proof.
Shoulder to shoulder, books file in like soldiers
to settle the literary territory
of one who has been seen as saint and monster.

One story goes back to Derry, New Hampshire, years
before England. Lesley was six or so.
In the middle of the night, she was awakened
by her father, who conducted her downstairs,
her feet cold on the floor. At the kitchen table
her mother wept, face hidden in her hands.
It was then that Lesley spotted the revolver.
"Take your choice," Frost said, as he waved the thing
between himself and Elinor – a less bracing
alternative than a poem unwritten yet
would give between two roads in a yellow wood.
"Before morning," he warned, "one of us will be dead."

The child was returned to bed. And only after
she'd tucked him in the earth would her memory
be brought to light – or fixed, at least, in print.
Was it true? Or a vivid, fluttering scarf of nightmare?
It wrapped, somehow, around the family neck.
For it wasn't Lesley, but her brother Carol
who – whether or not the grisly tale was real –
rewrote it with his life. It was the ninth
of October, 1940; he was thirty-eight.
He'd kept his own boy, Prescott, up for hours
with talk of his failures as a poet-farmer;

of fears (but here the doctors would be wrong –
his wife lived on for more than fifty years)
that Lillian might not even last the night.
When Prescott drifted off, he took the shotgun
he'd bought for Lillian as a wedding gift
and went downstairs, before the sun could rise,
to turn it on himself.

                Strange how in families
time seeps through all we do, so that the order
in which things happen seems to bow before
the dreamlike authority of metaphor.
Marjorie, the baby, dies in childbirth;
Elinor (who was "the unspoken half,"
Frost said, "of everything I ever wrote"–
if it wasn't true, one has no doubt he meant it)
is stricken at the heart while climbing stairs,
as if away from the scenes to come, when Carol
tep by step descends flights of despair,
and Irma's mind unravels in and out
of the hospital. Time spirals to rearrange
events to show us something beyond change.

"Two things are sure," Carol's father had written
to Lillian in the midst of a world war
in which, he thought, a man might best have died
a soldier. "He was driven distracted by life
and he was perfectly brave." And yet he runs
his hand across more pages, as if to smooth
the mound of a new grave: Carol's mind
was one, he writes this time, with a "twist from childhood."
Think how, the year before, he'd raced through stop-signs:
his eyes veered "off the road ahead too often."

Now Frost is eighty-eight. He can see ahead.
Poet of chance and choice, who tossed a coin
but knew which side his bread was buttered on,
who said, "The most inalienable right of man
is to go to hell in his own way," here he is
in a hospital bed, a hell he hasn't made.
He has a letter from Lesley, who knows him for
the stubborn vanities and selfless gestures.
She knows, dear girl, the words to make him well,
if anything can make him well. She calls him
"Robert Coeur de Lion." Too weak to write,
he dictates a final letter back to her.
"You're something of a Lesley de Lion
yourself," he says, and he commends the children's
poems she's been working on. It's good
to have a way with the young. The old man
hasn't lost his knack, even in prose,
for giving the truth the grandeur of a cadence.
"I'd rather be taken for brave than anything else."

*from*

# A Kiss in Space

(1999)

# Wreckage

Torn from the moorings of sleep
one morning, grasping not even a scrap
of whatever I was dreaming,

I realize, as I rise from the billowing
sail of the pillow, and sink again,
that I myself am wreckage

from the ship that smashed miraculously
the instant it broke
consciousness; am driftwood

toyed with at the edge of the tide,
a floating, disembodied arm
left to record the dream

it does not remember, while all the other
passengers heavily go down
to an oblivion where no

plumb line of a memory
of having had a memory
can reach. I alone on the beach

am real, and stand at last to fill
the funnel of the coffee filter
with spooned black heaps of sand,

watch as the hourglass spills the grains
of millions of associations
drop by drop in the O

of sentience that swells to a runnel,
smells like thought and is drinkable
and clarifies the thinking:

*Wreckage*

so early it's already too late
to say I never wanted to cross
into a wholly rational state,

to upend the coffee grounds like a sand
castle into the sink and rise
to the occasion of day, another

impermanent construction washed
down the drain; didn't want to dissolve
in the shower now these unseen cells

in the foam – little parts of the selves
I can't be part of anymore;
didn't want to walk away dry.

# A Rainbow over the Seine

Noiseless at first, a spray
of mist in the face, a nose-
gay of moisture never
destined to be a downpour.

Until the sodden cloud
banks suddenly empty
into the Seine with a loud
clap, then a falling ovation

for the undrenchable
sun – which goes on shining
our shoes while they're filling
like open boats and the sails

of our newspaper hats
are flagging, and seeing
that nobody thought to bring
an umbrella, puts

up a rainbow instead.
A rainbow over the Seine,
perfectly wrought as a draw-
bridge dreamed by a child ·

in crayon, and by the law
of dreams the connection
once made can only be lost;
not being children

we stand above the grate
of the Métro we're not
taking, thunder underfoot, and
soak up what we know:

the triumph of this *arc-*
*en-ciel,* the dazzle
of this monumental
prism cut by drizzle, is

that it vanishes.

# A Leak Somewhere

No toy in a bathtub, the Titanic;
but on our twenty-one-inch screen
it's faintly laughable, as Barbara Stanwyck
and her daughter in their lifeboat gasp
at the sight of the great vessel sliding
into the North Atlantic like a spoon.

Yet only faintly laughable.
When the ship blows up, with Stanwyck's son
and husband on it, the four of us
(warm beneath one blanket flung
across a comfy sofa in
the lifeboat of our living room)

bob with the waves of melodrama.
How ironic! Their family had split
even onboard, but along other lines:
living abroad had spoiled the girl
(Annette was so pretentious she
addressed her fellow Yanks in French),

but Norman, with his normal name,
might still be saved in Michigan.
Or that was Stanwyck's plan. And now
he's sinking with shallow Clifton Webb,
his Paris-besotted father, to
a depth where such distinctions are all

for naught. The ship's a symbol of
society, we tell our children –
belowdecks, into the porthole maws
of furnaces, bare-torsoed men
stoke coal until their sweat runs black;
when the iceberg slices through the hull,

they're flooded in an instant. Above
in steerage, the crammed-in families
of the kerchiefed, overexcitable poor
race for the door and, as water climbs,
scramble upstairs where Guggenheims
and Astors (so well-bred they barely

raise an eyebrow even for
historic personal disasters)
set down their hands of bridge, and don
life jackets like the latest fashion.
Not enough lifeboats? Noblesse oblige,
everybody at once is noble,

and an instinctive revolution
reshuffles the classes: women and children
first. Down the Jacob's ladder
of rope they struggle to the shaky
safety of going on living, while
those left behind on the heavenly

height of the tilting ship take solace
in their perfectly rehearsed rendition
of "Nearer, My God, to Thee."
Oh, you and I can laugh. But having
turned off the set, and led the kids
upstairs into dry beds, we sense

that hidden in the house a fine
crack – nothing spectacular,
only a leak somewhere – is slowly
widening to claim each of us
in random order, and we start to rock
in one another's arms.

# Video Blues

My husband has a crush on Myrna Loy,
and likes to rent her movies, for a treat.
It makes some evenings harder to enjoy.

The list of actresses who might employ
him as their slave is too long to repeat.
(My husband has a crush on Myrna Loy,

Carole Lombard, Paulette Goddard, coy
Jean Arthur with that voice as dry as wheat …)
It makes some evenings harder to enjoy.

Does he confess all this just to annoy
a loyal spouse? I know I can't compete.
My husband has a crush on Myrna Loy.

And can't a woman have her dreamboats? Boy,
I wouldn't say my life is incomplete,
but some evening I could certainly enjoy

two hours with Cary Grant as *my* own toy.
I guess, though, we were destined not to meet.
My husband has a crush on Myrna Loy,
which makes some evenings harder to enjoy.

# Home Movies: A Sort of Ode

Because it hadn't seemed enough,
after a while, to catalogue
more Christmases, the three-layer cakes
ablaze with birthday candles, the blizzard
Billy took a shovel to,
Phil's lawnmower tour of the yard,
the tree forts, the shoot-'em-ups
between the boys in new string ties
and cowboy hats and holsters,
or Mother sticking a bow as big
as Mouseketeer ears in my hair,

my father sometimes turned the gaze
of his camera to subjects more
artistic or universal:
long closeups of a rose's face;
a real-time sunset (nearly an hour);
what surely were some brilliant autumn
leaves before their colors faded
to dry beige on the aging film;
a great deal of pacing, at the zoo,
by polar bears and tigers caged,
he seemed to say, like him.

What happened between him and her
is another story. And just as well
we have no movie of it, only
some unforgiving scowls she gave
through terrifying, ticking silence
when he must have asked her (no
sound track) for a smile.
Still, what I keep yearning for
isn't those generic cherry
blossoms at their peak, or the brave
daffodil after a snowfall,

it's the re-run surprise
of the unshuttered, prefab blanks
of windows at the back of the house,
and how the lines of aluminum
siding are scribbled on with meaning
only for us who lived there;
it's the pair of elephant bookends
I'd forgotten, with the upraised trunks
like handles, and the books they meant
to carry in one block to a future
that scattered all of us.

And look: it's the stoneware mixing bowl
figured with hand-holding dancers
handed down so many years
ago to my own kitchen, still
valueless, unbroken. Here
she's happy, teaching us to dye
the Easter eggs in it, a Grecian
urn of sorts near which – a foster
child of silence and slow time
myself – I smile because she does
and patiently await my turn.

# Libretto

*Libretto*. That's the first Italian word
    she wants to teach me: "little book."
This afternoon (but why are we alone?
    Were Daddy and my brothers gone
all day, or has memory with its flair
    for simple compositions air-
brushed them from the shot?) she's set aside
    just for the two of us, and a lesson.

On an ivory silk couch that doesn't fit
    the life she's given in Detroit,
we gaze across the living room at the tall
    "European" drapes she's sewn
herself: a work of secret weights and tiers,
    hung after cursing at her own
mother's machine. She lets the needle fall
    onto the record's edge; then turns

to pull a hidden cord, and the curtain rises
    on Puccini's strings and our front view
of shut two-car garages, built for new
    marriages constructed since the war.
Well, not so new. It's 1962
    and though I'm only eight, I know
that with two cars, people can separate.
    He went away; came back for more

operatic scenes heard through the wall
    as if through a foreign language. Muffled
fury and accusation, percussive sobs:
    they aren't happy. Who couldn't tell
without the words? *Libretto*. On my knees
    the English text, the Italian on hers,
and a thrill so loud the coffee table throbs.
    I'm following her finger as

we're looping to a phrase already sung
    or reading four lines at a time
of people interrupting and just plain
    not listening, and yet the burden
of the words is simple: Butterfly must die.
    Pinkerton will betray her, though the theme
rippling above him like a hoisted flag
    is The Star-Spangled Banner. Mother, why

would a Japanese and an American
    sing Italian at each other?
Why would he get married and not stay?
    And have a child he'd leave to wait
with the mother by the screen with her telescope
    for the ship of hope? Why, if he knew
it wouldn't last, did he come back to Japan?
    – But I'm not asking her. *That's men*

is her tacit, bitter answer; was always half
    her lesson plan. *O say, can you see …*
yes, now I can. Your dagger's at the throat
    and yet I feel no rage; as tears
stream down our faces onto facing pages
    fluttering like wings, I see you meant
like Butterfly to tie a blindfold over
    a loved child's eyes: the saving veil of Art.

For it is only a story. When the curtain
    drops, our pity modulates
to relief she isn't us, and what's in store
    for you, divorce and lonely death,
remains distant. We have our nights to come
    of operas to dress up for,
our silly jokes, our shopping, days at home
    when nothing is very wrong and in my chair

I read some tragedy in comfort, even
    a half-shamed joy. You gave me that –
my poor, dear parents, younger thèn than I
    am now; with a stagestruck, helpless wish
that it wouldn't hurt and that it would, you made
    me press my ear against the wall
for stories that kept me near and far,
    and because the hurt was beautiful

even to try to write them; to find that living
    by stories is itself a life.
Forgive whatever artifice lies
    in my turning you into characters
in my own libretto – one sorry hand
    hovering above the quicksand
of a turntable in a house in Detroit
    I can't go back to otherwise.

# The Jewel of the World

1.

Lion and unicorn, with as sure
a sense of theater as saints
in paintings who flank Mary's throne,

or as circus animals
on hind legs – one paw wrapped around
a flagpole while another lifts

the curtain of a curious tent
paisleyed with golden, swimming tears –
open the magnificent

tapestry of a landscape rising
impossibly backstage in red:
a floral vertigo that rabbits

munch on in mid-air, while goats
and dogs and spread-winged falcons float
above the perennial thought of green.

Four trees planted in the ocean-
blue of the Lady's island spring
up like four seasons all at once

and forever. Flowering orange and oak,
holly and pine: each of them,
like her, is in its prime.

Set like a jewel in the oval
ring of her island, fabulous
in her studded headdress

(in the fashion of the day,
one stiff lock of braided hair
shoots up like a horn), the Lady

holds, in a kind of winding-sheet,
a necklace to be buried in
the casket in her servant's hands.

Gone is the life of senses she
had always kept in fine control;
she casts it off to save her soul.

But like a miniature of the trunk
a magician asks his volunteer
to enter so she may be sawn

in half, the jewel box leaves open
questions of renunciation.
Who could give away the world

undivided? Or at least
this one, a blooming hyperbole
of earthly beauty? A MON SEUL

DESIR, the legend reads above
her tent, which only makes it clear
that the desire to want no more

has always been too much to want.
We've kept this jewel of tapestry –
and swear she puts the necklace on.

2.

Step out from the Cluny and cross the Seine.
The bells are floating at Notre Dame, where sun
throws patterns from the scaffolding and swims
blind into the windows where it can.
The perpetual rose grows dirty and is cleaned
but never sheds a petal.

Nor, when you walk west along the quai,
watching the river splinter into stains
of painful brilliance, on to where the joined
pyramid of glass above the Louvre
flashes its hand, a diamond marrying
buried years to this one, will you find

a single way to turn your face from life –
nowhere in the museum's honeycomb
of centuries. There, within one niche
eternity gives to Titian, his *La mise
en tombeau* is lowering the priceless
body into its unseen vault again:

Jesus Christ, King of the Jews, the jewel
of the world. Held still by his ring
of mourners in a winding-sheet, his weight
is nearly more than anyone can bear.
Heaven and Earth. Son of God in eclipse,
head and torso blocked off by the shadow

cast by an enigma: Nicodemus,
Joseph of Arimathea, John the Baptist
half-seem to be lifting him into the light.
Going or coming? Mary Magdalene knows
nothing yet, as she turns the Virgin away,
of visions meant for her on the third day –

the stone gone from the sepulchre, the angels
waiting at head and foot, the man she weeps for
unrecognized until he speaks her name.
The story hangs from his suspended frame
only because we know it; have seen him rise
in other galleries, stepping from each tomb

as if from a refreshing bath.
Prolific Titian lovingly stroked more
farewells like these in light and shadow,
Christ's head at the right, then at the left;
one ends up at the Louvre, two at the Prado,
the world abloom with entombments.


3.
In Venice, sinking imperceptibly
each morning as the sun climbs from a sea
whose iridescence flakes into mosaics,

Titian has risen once again and turns
to his final canvas, the massive Pietà
meant for an altarpiece near his own grave.

Fierce Mary Magdalene, having cast off
her sinner's finery – even the jeweled tones
borrowed from Bellini – runs in, a smear

of army green descending from the left,
arm raised in grief, half as if she'd wave
us in and half away. What's to be done,

while the Virgin cradles uselessly the grown
son in her lap, but kneel to her and pray
(as does half-naked, ragged St. Jerome

or Job or Nicodemus or perhaps
Joseph of Arimathea – an old man,
in any case, identified as Titian)

and stare into the face of all our losses?
The master drops his brush, paints with bare hands.
Pearl of the late style, the head of Jesus

reclines into the lustrous oyster shell
of the temple apse, colder than the deepest
place in the ocean, a face so radiantly

cold, so terrifying, even Mary
holds him at a distance.
Titian also has a favorite son.

He has propped a votive panel – a little painting
within a painting, of Orazio
praying with his father – against one

of the pedestals with lions' faces raising
Moses and the Hellespontic sybil,
two prophets, to the level of the saints,

and under the cross-bearing sibyl's robes
has placed, horrifically, what even he
can't wholly comprehend: a severed hand.

Suspend your disbelief. It is the hand
passed on to Palma, who'll finish the Pietà
after Titian and his son fall to the plague.

Palma lifts his brush much like a needle
saving a dropped stitch, so that each thread
in the tapestry of loss is duly numbered,

much as the Lord counts hairs on every head
before he claims us, much as the attorney
catalogues, when thieves ransack the house

after Titian's death, what now exists
elsewhere: they took away, he writes, "things
of gold, silver and gems,

and innumerable paintings of great value."

# Distance

From up here, the insomniac
river turning in its bed
looks like a line somebody painted
so many years ago it's hard
to believe it was ever liquid; a motorboat
winks in the sun and leaves a wake
that seals itself in an instant, like the crack
in a hardly broken heart.

And the little straight-faced houses
that with dignity bear the twin
burdens of being unique and all alike,
and the leaf-crammed valley like the plate
of days that kept on coming and I ate
though laced with poison: I can look
over them, from this distance, with an ache
instead of a blinding pain.

Sometimes, off my guard, I half-
remember what it was to be
half-mad: whole seasons gone; the fear
a stranger in the street might ask
the time; how feigning normality
became my single, bungled task.
What made me right again? I wouldn't dare
to guess; was I let off

for good behavior? Praise
to whatever grace or power preserves
the living for living ... Yet I see the square
down there, unmarked, where I would pace
endlessly, and as the river swerves
around it, wonder what portion of
love I'd relinquish to ensure
I'd never again risk drowning.

# The Seven Weepers

The tines of his comb were splitting into finer
brittle strands, like hair, but his own hair –
deader than a corpse's, which can lengthen
in the sweet cool of the coffin – had stopped growing.
Screws unscrewed themselves from wooden boxes
where the stone-dry food was kept. Matches ignited
magically in air, as they fell to earth.
And who would believe it? When he took his pen
to paper, to record the temperature –
a hundred fifty-seven in the sun,
in the shade a hundred thirty-two – the ink
dried at the nib; the lead dropped whole from pencils.
What he had wanted was to draw a line
on the map from Adelaide into the heart
of the outback, where he'd willed a vast Australian
sea like the Caspian. But water holes
of a single shrinking creek were all they'd found,
like the globules of a burst thermometer.

Worst, he thought, was how the rising moon
offered no respite – so blinding that the black
swans that flew across its surface seemed
charred in the passage. Mostly, nothing moved
but ants and lizards. He who had fought
with Wellington against the French, who'd quelled
riots in Ireland, and headed a convict guard
all the way to the wrong end of the world,
where summer raged in January, now
had loitered with his men and bulls and horses
by a nameless pool, with debilitating wisdom,
six months for a drop of rain. In July it came.
And watered them enough to drag themselves
safely for a while across the blank
he named the Stony Desert, with a compass
that couldn't tell them when they should turn back

from infernal sandhills, burnished red, so hard
the horses left no track, as in a dream.
Twice they retrenched and shifted course when hope
of water dried up, shallow and absurd:
a pigeon diving steeply into shadow
that might be mud but wasn't; a clump of bush.
In November a seagull, five hundred miles from sea,
led them to a salt lake, purplish blue,
the color of Heaven.

                  What then was this scene
of misery they'd stumbled on? Years later
in England, nearly blind, Charles Sturt would wake
some mornings to that sight of seven naked
black men in a circle by the lake,
wailing and weeping. So profligate! he thought,
spending their grief like that. Who knew
when it would rain again, or if the sun
would bake away this pond of indigo
to nothing? Fools. Better save your tears.

Some in his group knew tribal words, and tried them.
What was the matter? A death? But all the words
were wrong, and the seven weepers seemed
as if they'd long forgotten what it meant
to have an answer. Inconsolable
is all they were. – Somewhere beyond the terror
he'd caused once, early on, in native eyes,
when he'd come bounding forward on his horse.
It wasn't the horse, exactly, but himself
dismounting from it: apparently they'd thought
white man and horse were one, a sort of Centaur.

And yet there were no Centaurs, no such creatures
ever in their heads: the thought now struck him

with the beating of the sun (or so the tale
would go if one retold it as one chose,
too far from 1845 to say
what any of them were) that these were men
wholly unlike himself. What songs they chanted
into the air could only evaporate,
though their chimeras – like the man-sized snake
and the red, preposterous kangaroo – were real.
*Hath the rain a father? Or who hath begotten*
*the drops of dew?* That voice, which thundered now
in the groping cloud of dust that was his mind –
where had it come from? – was of course the voice
of God in the whirlwind, chastising his servant.
And hadn't Job lost seven sons? What help
that fact was to him, he could hardly say,
but he stood there wrapped in silence while the naked
sinners wept, until he could remember
that Job had sat for seven days in silence
before he spoke.

        He didn't have a week
to wait for them; his handkerchief was a rag.
Charles Sturt, whose nation soon would drape its flag
over the weepers' country like a shroud,
reached from his Christian soul and in the heat
uselessly, kindly, gave them his overcoat.

# Absolute September

How hard it is to take September
straight – not as a harbinger
of something harder.

Merely like suds in the air, cool scent
scrubbed clean of meaning – or innocent
of the cold thing coldly meant.

How hard the heart tugs at the end
of summer, and longs to haul it in
when it flies out of hand

at the prompting of the first mild breeze.
It leaves us by degrees
only, but for one who sees

summer as an absolute,
Pure State of Light and Heat, the height
to which one cannot raise a doubt,

as soon as one leaf's off the tree
no day following can fall free
of the drift of melancholy.

# Marco Polo

Midafternoon, and both shades drawn
over open windows: the September sun,
bright but temperate, is diffused
as through a lantern. My child and I
are lying on top of the covers, reading.
She has her book and I have mine.

She can read silently. So I can't
say what's happening in her book,
or how far it takes her from our narrow
New England street where, days from now,
a yellow school bus will rumble back
to claim her. But the noise out there

at this moment – the grating of roller skates
and of other children's voices (*Marco
Polo! Marco Polo!*) clearly
doesn't enter her ears at all.
In my book, set in old Tennessee, the author –
or the narrator at least – seems to feel

that the lazy lineages of his tale,
the burials, marriages, repay
our interest just because family
is always interesting. And because
he thinks so he's right; or that's partly why.
Thinking so makes him write that way:

some clumsy scandal or other is nobler
simply by having been described
in clean, smooth blocks of paragraphs,
well-paced, well-chosen words, and with
an even-handedness we wish
we rose to, in life, more than fleetingly.

Marco Polo

A breeze through the pair of windows turns
one of the shades up like a page,
then the other. Nothing makes her stir,
little reader. I'm no match for her.
I find I'm picturing the blind-
folded boy on the street, his arms outstretched

for the bodies of voices (*Marco Polo!*
*Marco Polo!*) that circle and taunt him,
and though it's only a game, the sounds
drift to my windows with the heightened
importance of the half-understood.
My book hasn't lost me, exactly; it seems

it's succeeding in leading me away
from itself – as a parent does, or tries to –
with something of its tone in my head.
I've never loved her more than today.
Why this should be, or how long joy
is containable, or how far she'll travel

to shake me – all of this matters, but
I manage not to say it aloud;
following the thought, the room
darkens when the schoolday sun,
as if trying on a new jacket, slips
briefly into a cloud.

# Liam

He's down again, aswim in a dream
of milk, and Teresa who is far
too tired to go back to sleep goes back
to the table where she tests the nib
of her pen, like the nipple on a bottle.

Into a bottle of permanent ink
she dips her pen and begins to trace
over her pencil-marks on the face
of the spiral scrapbook the name they chose
for him who has never dreamed of a name.

It's *William,* like his father, but
she has only got as far as *Will*
(the doubled *l* another spiral
to the *Liam* they now call him), which
leaves her still three letters to spell

the man who's curled up in *I am.*
– The stranger in the crib who seems
longer each time they lift him out
and will find that while they named the story
it is his to write.

# A Kiss in Space

That the picture
in *The Times* is a blur
is itself an accuracy. Where
this has happened is so remote
that clarity would misrepresent
not only distance but our feeling
about distance: just as
the first listeners at the telephone
were somehow reassured to hear
static that interfered with hearing
(funny word, *static,* that conveys
the atom's restlessness), we're
not even now – at the far end
of the century – entirely ready
to look to satellites for mere

resolution. When the *Mir*
invited the first American
astronaut to swim in the pool
of knowledge with Russians, he floated
exactly as he would have in space
stations of our own: no lane
to stay in, no line to determine
the deep end, Norman Thagard
hovered on the ceiling something
like an angel in a painting
(but done without the hard
outlines of Botticelli; more
like a seraph's sonogram),
and turned to Yelena Kondakova
as his cheek received her kiss.

And in this
too the blur made sense: a kiss
so grave but gravity-free, untouched
by Eros but nevertheless
out of the usual orbit, must
make a heart shift focus. The very
grounding in culture (they gave him bread
and salt, as Grandmother would a guest
at her dacha; and hung the Stars
and Stripes in a stiff crumple
because it would not fall), the very
Russianness of the bear hugs was
dizzily universal: for who
knows how to signal anything
new without a ritual?

Not the kitchen-table
reader (child of the Cold War,
of 3 × 5 cards, carbon copies,
and the manila folder), who takes a pair
of scissors – as we do when the size
of some idea surprises – and clips
this one into a rectangle
much like her piece of toast. There:
it's saved, to think of later.
Yet it would be unfair
to leave her looking smug; barely
a teenager when she watched, on
her snowy TV screen, a man
seeming to walk on the moon, she's
learned that some detail –

Virtual Reality or email,
something inexplicable and
unnatural – is always cropping up
for incorporation in what's human.
What ought to make it manageable,
and doesn't quite, is the thought
of humans devising it. She'll
remember Norman Thagard in June,
when the *Mir* (meaning Peace: but how
imagine this without agitation?)
docks with the *Atlantis* (meaning
the island Plato mentioned first
and which, like him, did not disappear
without a splash), to shuttle
the traveler back home – or

to whatever Earth has become.

*from*

# Open Shutters

(2003)

# Trompe l'Oeil

All over Genoa
you see them: windows with open shutters.
Then the illusion shatters.

But that's not true. You knew
the shutters were merely painted on.
You knew it time and again.

The claim of the painted shutter
that it ever shuts the eye
of the window is an open lie.

You find its shadow-latches strike
the wall at a single angle,
like the stuck hands of a clock.

Who needs to be correct
more often than once a day?
Who needs real shadow more than play?

Inside the house, an endless
supply of clothes to wash.
On an outer wall it's fresh

paint hung out to dry –
shirttails flapping on a frieze
unruffled by any breeze,

like the words pinned to this line.
And the foreign word is a lie:
that second *l* in *l'oeil*

which only looks like an *l*, and is silent.

# The Accordionist

A whining chord of warning – the Métro's version
of Concert A – and we clear the sliding doors.
People take their seats as if assigned.
Some of them open paperbacks, like playbills,
with a formal air of expecting interruption.
Or as if the passengers themselves are actors
in a scene the stage directions might have called
*Passengers reading,* so that it scarcely matters
when they turn the page, or even if it's blank.

Enter a gypsy boy, who lurches forward
carrying an accordion, like a stagehand
awaiting orders where to set it down.
But when the doors wheeze shut, as if by reflex
his accordion too collapses, opens, closes
to the tune of "La Vie en Rose." He has no shoes.
Unlike the rest of us, dressed soberly
in solid colors, he's a brazen mess
of hand-me-down, ill-fitting plaids and paisleys.
He's barely old enough to be skipping school,
but no note of fear or shyness, or of shame,
shadows his face: it was years ago already
somebody taught him how to do this.

To entertain, that is – and in the coin
of the culture: an Edith Piaf song pumped
for all it's worth from the heartsore instrument
the audience links with soundtracks of old films,
as a loving camera climbs the Eiffel Tower.
But nobody is looking entertained.
They seem to be in some other kind of movie,
more modern, calling for unblinking eyes
(the actor's oldest trick for coaxing tears)

that no longer lead to tears. No words. Just chords
too grand to be specified. Or is it that?
Blank faces, maybe, standing in for blank
faces, much like wearing basic black.

The boy's still young enough he plays right through
the next stop – when he might have passed a cup –
and now, with a shrug, he segues crudely to
another chestnut: "Je Ne Regrette Rien."
My station's coming up. I start to rummage
furtively in my wallet, held as close
to heart as a hand of cards (of credit cards
luck dealt me); isolate a franc. And stand,
nearly tumbling into him, to drop
the object of my keen deliberation
into the filthy pocket of his jacket,
careful not to touch it. In a second
I stride out from the car to my next scene
on the platform, where I know to exit right
and up the stairs, out to the world of light.
I'll never see him again.

But some instinct (as the train accelerates
and howls into the tunnel on its pleated
rubber joints, one huge accordion)
tells me to look back – a backward take
on Orpheus, perhaps, in which now only
Eurydice goes free? And fleetingly
I catch through windows of the next three cars
the boy repeated. No, these are his brothers –
each with an accordion in hand
and each boy inches taller than the last –
who handed down to him these blurring clothes,

and yet because the train unreels as fast
as a movie, a single window to a frame,
my eye's confused, has fused them as one boy
growing unnaturally, an understudy
condemned to play forever underground.

# Advent

Wind whistling, as it does
in winter, and I think
nothing of it until

it snaps a shutter off
her bedroom window, spins
it over the roof and down

to crash on the deck in back,
like something out of Oz.
We look up, stunned – then glad

to be safe and have a story,
characters in a fable
we only half-believe.

Look, in my surprise
I somehow split a wall,
the last one in the house

we're making of gingerbread.
We'll have to improvise:
prop the two halves forward

like an open double door
and with a tube of icing
cement them to the floor.

Five days until Christmas,
and the house cannot be closed.
When she peers into the cold

interior we've exposed,
she half-expects to find
three magi in the manger,

a mother and her child.
She half-expects to read
on tablets of gingerbread

a line or two of Scripture,
as she has every morning
inside a dated shutter

on her Advent calendar.
She takes it from the mantel
and coaxes one fingertip

under the perforation,
as if her future hinges
on not tearing off the flap

under which a thumbnail picture
by Raphael or Giorgione,
Hans Memling or David

of apses, niches, archways,
cradles a smaller scene
of a mother and her child,

of the lidded jewel-box
of Mary's downcast eyes.
*Flee into Egypt*, cries

the angel of the Lord
to Joseph in a dream,
*for Herod will seek the young*

*child to destroy him*. While
she works to tile the roof
with shingled peppermints,

I wash my sugared hands
and step out to the deck
to lug the shutter in,

a page torn from a book
still blank for the two of us,
a mother and her child.

# Erasers

As punishment, my father said, the nuns
    would send him and the others
out to the schoolyard with the day's erasers.

Punishment? The pounding symphony
    of padded cymbals clapped
together at arm's length overhead

(a snow of vanished alphabets and numbers
    powdering their noses
until they sneezed and laughed out loud at last)

was more than remedy, it was reward
    for all the hours they'd sat
without a word (except for passing notes)

and straight (or near enough) in front of starched
    black-and-white Sister Martha,
like a conductor raising high her chalk

baton, the only one who got to talk.
    Whatever did she teach them?
And what became of all those other boys,

poor sinners, who had made a joyful noise?
    My father likes to think,
at seventy-five, not of the white-on-black

chalkboard from whose crumbled negative
    those days were never printed,
but of word-clouds where unrecorded voices

gladly forgot themselves. And that he still
    can say so, though all the lessons,
most of the names, and (he doesn't spell

this out) it must be half the boys themselves,
  who grew up and dispersed
as soldiers, husbands, fathers, now are dust.

# Hare

At odd times, harum-scarum,
after we haven't seen him
        for a week or so, he hops
    from the bushes at stage right
onto our green proscenium.

Why do I say it's ours?
At best, I'm just a warden,
        standing with hands in suds
    at the kitchen window when
he breaks out of his warren.

Jittery, hunted vagrant,
he leaps as fast as Aesop
        claimed his kind could leap,
    then stops still in the grass
merely because it's fragrant –

a wholly interested,
systematic sensualist,
        a silent, smooth lawn mower
    that hardly can go slower.
Sometimes he gets ahead

(or tries to) with the jet set,
in a long line at the airport
        pulling his legs behind him
    like luggage, bit by bit –
the nametag of his scut

attached at the last minute.
Meanwhile, I stay put
        inside the house we bought
    a year ago, a new
woman at the window –

but of that he has no clue,
now pawn, now skipping knight
        on sun-squares on the lawn,
    while dreaming the old dream
a hare has, of his harem.

    Is he in fact the same
animal all the time?
        In my way promiscuous
    as he, how could I swear
he's not some other hare

    that pauses blank-eyed, poses
as if for praise, and then,
        rather than jump over,
    inserts himself within
a low bush, like a lover?

    Both of us bad at faces,
mere samples of our species,
        will either of us be missed?
    The dishes in my hands
are shards for the archeologist.

# Deliveries Only

*for Sarah Marjorie Lyon, born in a service elevator*

Your whole life long, you'll dine
out on the same questions:
*In your building? On what floor?*
*Was it going up or down?*

They'll need the precise location –
*Seventy-ninth and Lex? –*
as if learning it could shield them
from the consequences of sex.

*Wasn't your mother a doctor?*
*Didn't she talk him through*
*how to do it?* And then you'll tell them
how your father delivered you,

that only after your birth
did he think to reach in her bag
and dial 911.
He held you up like a phone

and was taught how to cut the cord.
*What about proper hygiene?*
*When did the ambulance come?*
Waiting, you were the siren,

squalling in a rage
behind the old-fashioned mesh
of the elevator door:
a Lyon cub in her cage.

*Didn't your parents worry?*
*Hadn't they done Lamaze?*
But you'll only shrug at your story:
*That was the way it was.*

# A Morris Dance

Across the Common, on a lovely May
day in New England, I see and hear
the Middle Ages drawing near,
bells tinkling, pennants bright and gay –
    a parade of Morris dancers.

One plucks a lute. One twirls a cape.
Up close, a lifted pinafore
exposes cellulite, and more.
O why aren't they in better shape,
    the middle-aged Morris dancers?

Already it's not hard to guess
their treasurer – her; their president – him;
the Wednesday night meetings at the gym.
They ought to practice more, or less,
    the middle-aged Morris dancers.

Short-winded troubadours and pages,
milkmaids with osteoporosis –
what really makes me so morose is
how they can't admit their ages,
    the middle-aged Morris dancers.

Watching them gamboling and tripping
on Maypole ribbons like leashed dogs,
then landing, thunderously, on clogs,
I have to say I feel like skipping
    the middle-aged Morris dancers.

Yet bunions and receding gums
have humbled me; I know my station
as a member of their generation.
Maybe they'd let me play the drums,
    the middle-aged Morris dancers.

# Another Session

### 1.

You opened with the rules. Outside this room
nothing I said inside would be repeated
unless in your best judgment I posed harm
to myself or others. It was like being read
my rights in some film noir – but I was glad
already I'd at last turned myself in,
guilty of anxiety and depression.

And worse. Confess it: worse. Of narcissist
indifference to how other people felt.
 Railing against myself, making a list
of everything (I thought), I'd left a fault
unturned: the one of needing to be praised
for forcing these indictments from my throat.
For saying them well. For speaking as I wrote.


### 2.

Not that the goal was chalking up demerits.
Indeed, I hoped you were basically on my side.
That's how I interpreted your nod,
your pleasant face (at first, a little hard
to judge behind that beard), your intelligent
air of listening further than I meant.
And never falsely, just to raise my spirits,
but because you couldn't not be interested.

"You writers!" When the outburst came, I started
out of my chair. (I'd had a habit then –
feet on your coffee table. Never again.)
"This is real life. You don't live in a novel.
People aren't characters. They're not a symbol."
We stared, stunned at the other, stony-hearted.

3.

Once or twice a week, for a year. But ten
years ago already, so that today
those intimate, subtle, freeform sessions shrink
to memorized refrains: "You seem to think
people can read your mind. You have to *say*" –
itself said kindly – or that time you accused me
of picturing love too much like "Barbie and Ken.
Why does it have to be all youth and beauty?"

Therapists have themes, as writers do.
(A few of mine, then: the repertoire includes
clocks, hands, untimely death, snow-swollen clouds.)
Like it or not, I picked up more from you:
No showing off. In failure, no surprise.
Gratitude. Trust. Forgiveness. Fantasies.


4.

The last time I saw your face – how far back now? –
was when I took my daughters (I still don't
know what possessed me) to a "family restaurant."
Dinosaur portions, butter enough to drown
all sorrows in, cakes melded from candy bars ...
Having filed you away for years and years,
suddenly I was nervous, my life on show.
*I'm still married, thanks. Husband's out of town.*

But there was no talking to you across the aisle
where, by some predestined trick of seating,
your brood in its entirety was eating
(their dinners, I suppose, were just as vile)
with backs to me, remaining as they must
faceless to patients even from the past.

5.

*Killed instantly.* That's what a mutual friend
told me when I asked how it had happened.
*Good,* I said, *I'm glad he didn't suffer –*
each of us reaching (not far) for a phrase
from a lifetime stock of journalists' clichés
which, we had learned, provide a saving buffer
within our bifurcated selves: the one
that's horrified; the one that must go on.

Killed in a bicycle race. I've scrapped the Wheel
of Fortune, the Road of Life. No, this is real,
there's no script to consult: you've lost your body.
Still having one, I pace, I stretch, I cough,
I wash my face. But then I'm never ready.
This is the sonnet I've been putting off.


6.

And also this one, in which your fancy bike
hits a concrete barrier and you fly
over it into fast *oncoming traffic –*
the obituary's formula for one man
driving a truck, who didn't even have
time to believe the corner of his eye,
until the thing was done, and he must live
always as if this nightmare were the one
deed he was born to do and to relive,
precisely the sort of person you would trust
in fifty-minute sessions to forgive
himself, to give himself at least two years
of post-traumatic whatsit to adjust
to thoughts of all those people left in tears.

7.

Only once did you confide a story
from your own life. (And only to illustrate
how long "people" take to overcome a shock.)
An accident – you broke your neck? Your back?
Shameful I don't remember – and for three
years you'd take a detour to avoid
the sight of it: that swinging, high red light
somebody ran, that road that crossed a road.

A run-through of the sped-up, drawn-out second
of terror before your second, actual end.
Swinging past the turnoff to your clinic
today, I saw I'd never choose to drive
that street again; would steer around the panic
rather than fail to find you there alive.


8.

Notice – but you can't – I don't write your name.
*People aren't characters.* Here's my concession
(small) to that view, and your need of privacy
which, I suspect, went beyond your profession.
When I knew you – no, you knew *me* – I'd missed the easy
truth we had acquaintances in common.
(A good thing, probably, I'd been too dim
to ask you; you too classy to let on.)

Nor did I find the public facts in print
(*age 53, father of three, an active
member of his church*) until you'd long
been dead. That July I came and went.
You reached me in a place I don't belong –
seventeen months later, Christmas Eve.

9.

I'd got there early, casually saved a front
pew for the whole family with some flung
mittens and hats. (In gestures we assume
the shoulder-to-shoulder permanence of home.)
Shouldn't we come more often? "The Power of Love":
our sermon. A list called "Flowers in Memory of"
on the program's final page. I was feeling faint.
Your name. Your father's name? Something was wrong.

I knew it was you. The church was going black.
Head down: my first anxiety attack
since the bad old days. Your face at the restaurant.
My plate heaped up with food I didn't want.
Keep the head down. People would be saying
to themselves (and close enough) that I was praying.

10.

Revise our last encounter. I'd rather say
it was that day a decade ago we made
a formal farewell: I was going away
on a long trip. If I needed you, I said,
when I got back, I'd be sure to give a call.
You stood up, and I finally saw how tall
you were; I'd never registered how fit.
Well, all we'd done for a year was talk and sit.

*Paris,* you said. Then, awkwardly, *Lucky you.*
Possessor of my secrets, not a friend,
colder, closer, our link unbreakable.
Yet we parted better than people often do.
We looked straight at each other. Was that a smile?
I thanked you for everything. You shook my hand.

# For Emily at Fifteen

*Sirens living in silence, why would they leave the sea?*
          – Emily Leithauser

Allow me one more try,
though you and I both know
you're too old now to need
writing about by me –

you who composed a sonnet
and enclosed it in a letter,
casually, with family news,
while I was away;

who rummaged in convention's
midden for tools and symbols
and made with them a maiden
voyage from mere verse

into the unmapped world
of poetry. A mermaid
(like Eve, you wrote – a good
analogy, and yet

your creature acts alone)
chooses to rise from wordless
unmindful happiness
up to the babbling surface

of paradox and pain.
I whose job it's been
to protect you read my lesson:
you'll wriggle from protection.

Half-human and half-fish
of adolescence, take
my compliments, meant half
as from a mother, half

one writer to another,
for rhymes in which you bury
ironies – for instance,
*sirens* into *silence;*

and since I've glimpsed a shadow,
forgive how glad I felt
when I set down your sonnet
to read your letter again

with only silliness in it,
the old tenth-grade bravado:
"Oh well, I bombed the chem test.
Latin's a yawn a minute."

# Midsummer, Georgia Avenue

Happiness: a high, wide porch, white columns
crowned by the crepe-paper party hats
of hibiscus; a rocking chair; iced tea; a book;
an afternoon in late July to read it,
or read the middle of it, having leisure
to mark the place and enter it tomorrow
just as you left it (knock-knock of woodpecker
keeping yesterday's time, cicada's buzz,
the turning of another page, and somewhere
a question raised and dropped, the pendulum-
swing of a wind chime). Back and forth, the rocker
and the reading eye, and isn't half

your jittery, odd joy the looking out
now and again across the road to where,
under the lush allées of long-lived trees
conferring shade and breeze on those who feel
none of it, a hundred stories stand confined,
each to their single page of stone? Not far,
the distance between you and them: a breath,
a heartbeat dropped, a word in your two-faced
book that invites you to its party only
to sadden you when it's over. And so you stay
on your teetering perch, you move and go nowhere,
gazing past the heat-struck street that's split

down the middle – not to put too fine
a point on it – by a double yellow line.

# Peonies

Heart-transplants my friend handed me:
four of her own peony bushes
in their fall disguise, the arteries
of truncated, dead wood protruding
from clumps of soil fine-veined with worms.

"Better get them in before the frost."
And so I did, forgetting them
until their June explosion when
it seemed at once they'd fallen in love,
had grown two dozen pink hearts each.

Extravagance, exaggeration,
each one a girl on her first date,
excess perfume, her dress too ruffled,
the words he spoke to her too sweet –
but he was young; he meant it all.

And when they could not bear the pretty
weight of so much heart, I snipped
their dew-sopped blooms; stuffed them in vases
in every room like tissue-boxes
already teary with self-pity.

*from*

# A Phone Call to the Future

(2008)

# Wake-Up Call

The water is slapping *wake up, wake up,* against the boat
chugging away from Venice, infinite essence
of what must end because it is beautiful,

Venice that shrinks to a bobbing, pungent postcard
and then to nothing at all as the automatic
doors at the airport obligingly shut behind you.

Re-enter a world where everything's much the same,
where you've gone slack again, and don't even know it,
so unaware that you actually shrug to yourself,

*I'll be back,* and yes, for some lucky stiffs it's true,
sometimes it's you, you're sure to get more chances
at Venice, and Paris, and that blessed, unmarked place

where you sat on a bench and he kissed you that first time,
so many kisses, you hoped he would never stop,
you can hope, at least, not ever to forget it,

or forget how your babies, latching onto your breast,
would roll up their eyes in an ecstasy that was comic
in its seriousness, though your joy was no less grave,

but you're not going back to so much, and more and more,
the longer you live there's more not to go back to,
and what you demand in your gratitude and greed

is more life in which to get so attached to something,
someone or someplace, you're sure you'll die right then
when you can't have it back, something you don't even know

the name of yet, but will be yours before receding
as an indispensable ache; what you're saying
is *Lord, surprise me with even more to miss.*

# Lunar Eclipse

*in memory of Anthony Hecht*

Days after you died,
when your face was everywhere
I turned (craggy, inclined

to be reflective, kindly, in
parentheses of pure
white hair and white goatee),

a lunar eclipse, the last
we'd see for years, was promised,
and I took a kitchen chair,

a pencil, and a notebook
out to the moonstruck driveway,
knowing you'd be there.

A shadow-boxer's blow
had caught the moon's left jaw;
in silence and slow motion

it crept up, a gloved fist
of darkness that kept looming.
In saddened admiration

I watched the giant fail –
a dimming, a diminution,
among the attendant stars.

Dark poet, you were called.
Your last poems were in keeping
with that judgment; gave a world

where "no joy goes unwept."
Yet the act of making
was light and lightness still

when a man of eighty-one
immortalized the sun
on his wife's face as she slept.

I stayed out late, in hope
such clear skies would provide
a luminary's comeback,

a rematch with itself.
And friends told me they saw it.
As for our moon, a sudden

cloud – a blanket pulled
over the vanquished head
of one on his deathbed –

was my signal to go in.
Not enough light to write by.
Later, I would try.

# Costanza Bonarelli

A bust that looks just-kissed,
from the blind intensity
of her gaze to the somewhat swollen
parted lips, to the parting,
   above her rumpled chemise,
of two soft breasts his hands
   lifted from stone, Bernini's

lover was designed
to please – to have and hold
in his own eyes as forever
undone and to-be-done-to,
   a melting readiness.
Oh the inconstant Costanza,
   true-to-life but untrue! –

whose drawing power, coiled
as the heavy braid he pulled
behind her head, yet loose
as the involving tendrils
   that tumbled to one side,
originated from
   within a designing woman.

If either alone suffices
(love or art, that is)
to lead a man to believe
whole days can be best spent
   lost in a woman's hair,
how could he not have wept
   at the upswept and downfallen

tresses of one who was
both singular ideal –
a thing he'd hewn from rock
into his own landmark
in portraiture, quintessence
of the sinuous baroque –
and all too two-faced mistress?

That she was capable
of deception – this was fine,
one guesses: a frisson
at first, that she (the wife
of his apprentice) gave
in private no resistance
to a greater man's assistance.

But now the great man's brother?
His brother? When the rumor
reached him, Bernini sent
a razor-bearing servant
to do what must be done.
He wasn't going to kill her.
No, but he'd leave a scar,

a sort of *Kilroy was here;*
he'd affix his stamp, he'd fix her
once and for all, for good –
indeed, he'd have his thug
underling slash her face,
her living flesh, with a tool
not so unlike the one

that he alone, the master,
had been skilled enough to wield,
watching the marble yield
to each sweet, painstaking stroke
of chisel against cheek
until, so real, she fairly
cried out for more.

# Goodbye, Train

I'm stepping off the train behind a pair
of thirtysomethings with their baby daughter.

The father will stay fit for years, I think,
though here and there, his hair's a little thin;

the mother's confident in new blue jeans
she knows are sexy – but carefully, tastefully so.

Seeing them floods me at once – I can't say why –
with solicitude. Delight, and envy. Pain.

"Goodbye, train," the mother says, and then,
"Say 'goodbye, train,' 'bye bye.' " She waves her hand

theatrically, the way we often will
with children, so that nobody can find us

guilty, ourselves, of any silliness –
of joy in the trainman's cap, his ticket-punch.

The little girl is propped on her father's hip
and pointing vaguely at a world of things

she's just come to know, and which now must go away.
How grave she seems! – a toothless oracle.

I see too how I look, if anyone's looking:
a weathered niceness, a trudging competence.

That's how I follow, twenty years ahead
of the parents, as I lug my bags behind them,

vowing to keep a stranger's proper distance –
as I did from those two lovesick teenagers

clinging in tears some stations back, when he
prepared himself to be left there on the platform

by a girl who swore it wasn't possible,
and both were stunned to discover that it was.

I think what luck it is, to be one who says
goodbye to trains instead of other people.

# Executive Shoeshine

It may go on snowing forever,
but meanwhile, how he's basking
in the sun of his own multitasking!
He's perched erect on his throne
looking down on the airport food court,
as the silver snail of a cell phone
earpiece hooked to his ear
hangs on his every word.
No way to cut him short
until the runways are cleared
and they've finished out there de-icing
the right wing, then the left wing
of all those planes before his.
Could he strike us a deal with the weather?
The man hunched below him polishes
one wingtip, then the other.

# Poetry Slalom

Much less
the slam
than the slalom
gives me a thrill:
that solemn, no-fuss
Olympian skill
in skirting flag after flag
of the bloody obvious;
the fractional
lag,
while speeding downhill,
at the key
moment,
in a sort of whole-
body trill:
the note repeated,
but elaborated,
more touching and more
elevated
for seeming the thing
to be evaded.

# Aurora Borealis

An arc of searchlight
and, as such, a not quite
accurate
way of going about it:

if you were looking
for some lost thing
in the ring
of dark circling

the earth,
if the path
of light you hunted with
(emerging from underneath

the horizon, and trained
not by you but a hand
unseen) ended
with a sideways bend,

if its torch forked
and flickered
as if overworked,
if it torqued

inside itself with a wow
and a flutter, a now
you see it now
you don't, how

long would it take
before you'd make
the leap? – Would you look
at those freak

streaks in the sky
forever before saying, "I
see the light:
this *is* what I sought tonight"?

# A Phone Call to the Future

1.

Who says science fiction
is only set in the future?
After a while, the story that looks least
believable is the past.
The console television with three channels.
Black-and-white picture. Manual controls:
the dial clicks when you turn it, like the oven.
You have to get up and walk somewhere to change things.
You have to leave the house to mail a letter.

Waiting for letters. The phone rings: you're not there.
You'll never know. The phone rings, and you are,
there's only one, you have to stand or sit
plugged into it, a cord
confines you to the room where everyone
is also having dinner.
Hang up the phone. The family's having dinner.

Waiting for dinner. You bake things in the oven.
Or Mother does. That's how it always is.
She sets the temperature: it takes an hour.

The patience of the past.
The typewriter forgives its own mistakes.
You type on top sheet, carbon, onion skin.
The third is yours, a record of typeovers,
clotted and homemade-looking, like the seams
on dresses cut out on the dining table.
The sewing machine. The wanting to look nice.
Girls who made their dresses for the dance.

2.

This was the Fifties: as far back as I go.
Some of it lasted decades.
That's why I remember it so clearly.

Also because, as I lie in a motel room
sometime in 2004, scrolling
through seventy-seven channels on my back
(there ought to be more – this is a cheap motel room),
I can revisit evidence, hear it ringing.
My life is movies, and tells itself in phones.

The rotary phone, so dangerously languid
and loud when the invalid must dial the police.
The killer coming up the stairs can hear it.
The detective ducks into a handy phone booth
to call his sidekick. Now at least there's touch tone.
But wait, the killer's waiting in the booth
to try to strangle him with the handy cord.
The cordless phone, first noted in the crook
of the neck of the secretary
as she pulls life-saving files.
Files come in drawers, not in the computer.
Then funny computers, big and slow as ovens.
Now the reporter's running with a cell phone
larger than his head,
if you count the antenna.

They're Martians, all of these people,
perhaps the strangest being the most recent.
I bought that phone. I thought it was so modern.
Phones shrinking year by year, as stealthily
as children growing.

3.

It's the end of the world.
Or people are managing, after the conflagration.
After the epidemic. The global thaw.
Everyone's stunned. Nobody combs his hair.
Or it's a century later, and although
New York is gone, and love, and everyone
is a robot or a clone, or some combination,

you have to admire the technology of the future.
When you want to call somebody, you just think it.
Your dreams are filmed. Without a camera.
You can scroll through the actual things that happened,
and nobody disagrees. No memory.
No point of view. None of it necessary.

Past the time when the standard thing to say
is that, no matter what, the human endures.
That whatever humans make of themselves
is therefore human.
Past the transitional time
when humanity as we know it was there to say that.
Past the time we meant well but were wrong.
It's less than that, not anymore a concept.
Past the time when mourning was a concept.

Of course, such a projection,
however much I believe it, is sentimental –
belief being sentimental.
The thought of a woman born
in the fictional Fifties.

That's what I mean. We were Martians. Nothing's stranger
than our patience, our humanity, inhumanity.
Our worrying about robots. Earplug cell phones

that make us seem to be walking about like loonies
talking to ourselves. Perhaps we are.

All of it was so quaint. And I was there.
Poetry was there; we tried to write it.

*from*

# Nothing by Design

(2013)

# Common Room, 1970

*And Jesus said unto them, Come ye after me; and I will make*
*you to become fishers of men.*

– Mark 1.17

It was the age of sit-ins
and in any case, there weren't enough chairs.
The guys loped heavy-footed down the stairs
or raced each other to the bottom, laughing,
pushing their luck. But here they all crammed in,
sophomores, born like him in '51,
to huddle on the floor of the Common Room.

In a corner, a grandfather clock
startled the hour; hammered it home again.
He would remember that. The old New England
rickety dignity of the furniture.
The eminent, stern faces looking down
from time-discolored portraits. Or maybe some
of this was embellishment, added later on.

The flickering, thick fishbowl
of a TV screen, a Magnavox console,
silenced them all. There, in black and white,
gray-haired men in gray suits now began
to pull blue capsules from an actual fishbowl.
(At least the announcer said they were bright blue.)
It was the age of drugs. These looked like giant

Quaaludes handed out
by a mad pharmacist, whose grimly poised
assistant – female, sexless – then unscrewed
from each a poisonous slip of sticky paper.
A man affixed that date to a massive chart.
It was filling up already. (Some poor dude
named Bert was 7; he punched a sofa cushion.)

As for himself, he thought
of penny candy in a jar a million
years ago, picked out with his brother
most days after school. Or times he'd draw
tin soldiers from the bottom of a stocking.
(Born two days past Christmas, he'd always seen
that as good karma: the whole world free to play.)

A congressman was rifling
loudly through capsules, seized some in his fist,
dropped all but one. Not Jeremy? Good friend,
socked with 15. Two strangers, 38.
Ben got 120. Would that be good enough?
Curses, bluster, unfunny humor, crossed
fingers for blessed numbers that remained.

Somewhere, sometime in
that ammunition pile awaited his:
239. He heard the number whizz,
then lodge safe as a bullet in his brain.
Like a bullet in a dream: you're dead, you're fine.
No need to wish for C.O. or 4-F.
Oh thank you, Jesus God. No Nam for him.

Yet he was well brought up.
In decency, rather than dance for joy
or call up Mom right then from the hallway phone,
he stayed until the last guy knew his fate.
Typical Roy, who'd showed up late, freaked out
when, it appeared, his birthday got no mention.
He hadn't heard: they'd hosed him. Number 2.

*Common Room, 1970*


      Before the war was lost
some four years later, a handful in that room
would battle inside fishbowls, most in color –
and little men, toy soldiers in a jungle,
bled behind the glass while those excused,
life-sized, would sit before it eating dinner.
He'd lived to be a watcher. And number 2

      in the Common Room that day?
Clearly not stupid. Roy became a major
in Independent Projects. Something about
landscapes in oil, angles of northern sun.
By the time he graduated, he had won
a study grant to paint in England, where
(so his proposal went) the light was different.

# Fractal

A fish-shaped school of
fish, each individual
shaped like a single

scale on the larger
fish: some truths are all
a matter of scale,

in the manner that shale
will flake into thin layers
of and like itself,

or a roof is made
of shingle upon shingle
of roofish monad.

Scale, fish, school of fish…
"That's a fractal, isn't it?"
was your feedback when

you ate what I said.
"A form that's iterated:
output is input

ad infinitum."
Must I now mull it over?
I mulled it over.

This aquarium,
I thought, was a sort of think
tank for non-thinkers

in their open-mouthed
safety-in-numbers forage,
needing no courage.

Yet so beautiful:
mathematically serving
one end while swerving

in a fraction of
a second into action:
how do they sense when

to advance or back-
track, tail that guy, or swallow
the law to follow?

Somewhat in the line
of Leibnitz, Mandelbrot coined
the term *fractal*: it's

the hall-of-mirrors
parthenogenesis of
a recursive, nonce,

anonymously
irregular form: i.e.,
copies no other

formula can make.
(I learned that when I got home.)
An eye on either

side of a flat head
is useful, I read; herring
have a keen sense of hearing,

but it's not that that
gives them their unerring
"high polarity,"

pooling together
just close enough to discern
skin on a neighbor,

far enough to skirt
collision. That's a vision
scaled for fish – but what

human can marshal
acceptance, much less a wish,
for sight so partial?

"Stand back from the glass,
make room for the universe,"
I thought then; "at least

for whatever we
can compass: iteration
on iteration,

until fish fill the ocean."

# The Gods

I always seem to have tickets
in the third or fourth balcony
(a perch for irony;
a circle of hell the Brits
tend to call 'the gods'),
and peer down from a tier
of that empyrean

at some tuxedoed insect
scrabbling on a piano.
Some nights there's a concerto,
and ranks of sound amass
until it's raining upward
(violin-bows for lightning)
from a black thundercloud.

A railing has been installed
precisely at eye level –
which leads the gaze, frustrated,
still higher to the vault
of the gilt-encrusted ceiling,
where a vaguely understood
fresco that must be good

shows nymphs or angels wrapped
in windswept drapery.
Inscribed like the gray curls
around the distant bald spot
of the eminent conductor,
great names – DA VINCI PLATO
WHITTIER DEBUSSY –

form one long signature,
fascinatingly random,
at the marble base of the dome.
It's more the well-fed gods
of philanthropy who seem
enshrined in all their funny,
decent, noble, wrong

postulates, and who haunt
these pillared concert halls,
the tinkling foyers strung
with chandeliered ideals,
having selected which
dated virtues – COURAGE
HONOR BROTHERHOOD – rated

chiseling into stone;
having been quite sure
that virtue was a thing
all men sought, the sublime
a mode subliminally
fostered by mentioning
monumentally.

All men. Never a woman's
name, of course, although
off-shoulder pulchritude
gets featured overhead –
and abstractions you might go
to women for, like BEAUTY
JUSTICE LIBERTY.

*The Gods*

Yet at the intermission,
I generally descend
the spiral stairs unjustly
for a costly, vacant seat
I haven't paid for. Tonight
I've slipped into D9.
The lights dim. Warm applause

and, after a thrilling pause,
some stiff-necked vanities
for a moment float away –
all the gorgeous, nameless,
shifting discordances
of the world cry aloud; allowed
at last, I close my eyes.

# Our Friends the Enemy

*Christmas, 1914*

Were they mad?
They kicked the severed head
of the football across the frozen mud
like Ajax running wild in the field:
it was sheep he killed
when he'd thought he'd been slaughtering
Odysseus and Agamemnon.

Now it was either the war to end
all wars, or Armageddon,
but surely they'd been out of their wits
picking their way across No Man's Land
unarmed but for brandy and cigarettes
and pictures of girls they liked.
In no time the chaps with cameras
were snapping photographs –
Tommy swapping his cap for the spiked
Pickelhaube on Fritz.

*It started, Colonel, the night before.*
*Sir, I can explain…*
The Jerrys who wanted them dead so close
all along the front
they could hear them clear
as the stars, singing "Stille Nacht."
Some of the boys sang back:
"O Come All Ye Faithful."
A friendly taunt:
*"Engländer! Engländer!"*
And all ablaze,
the candles in rows
on the Germans' Christmas trees.

How did they dare walk across?
They'd trod their way through worse before –
lads underfoot in the muck;
now the day was cold enough those poor
contorted stiffs
were coated in merciful rime.

As for them, whose time
hadn't come, you could say that squalor
was the better part of valor.
You could call it a sort of luck
not standing in standing slime in the trench.
Not fraternizing with the rats
but clambering over the parapets
with a few of your rations in hand.

Sergeant Bernard Joseph Brookes
of the Queen's Westminster Rifles
wrote in his diary:
*In the afternoon I went out*
*and had a chat*
*with our friends the Enemy.*

And the football game?
It was a sort of courtship
before the first, last, passionate fusion.
Or it felt like the smiling sorrow
after you and your girl have split up.
But nothing forgiven, furious, tomorrow.

The Germans won, 3 to 2.

On Boxing Day
the mercury rose, and the mud.
It was agreed –

let the dead bury their dead –
and side by side, they dug.
They laid them in who hadn't played
but had already lost:

each a tidy Christmas package
tied with a cross.

# Nora

Even in death your radiance follows me.
Or leads me. You're ahead of me on the sidewalk,
pushing your baby's pram as I push mine,
and you swing your head to greet someone driving by,
your sheet of black hair the shiniest anyone
has ever seen; you don't even understand
that nobody in her thirties shines that much,

nobody laughs so musically at jokes
that are not that funny. Whatever it was I said
twenty years ago, whatever anyone said
no longer is heard, or can be, the way you took it
because you're not here to beam it back, to turn it
funny or beautiful – even the saddest things
you somehow made useful to us who were sad

with those infinite eyes of yours, looking right at us,
that *Oh* that was all acceptance. Even in death
that swept down upon you, death that locked you shut
and the *No* that is locked inside your name now, Nora,
I see the *Ra* for sun-god, too, which is silly,
but you'd understand; I take it for your radiance
that even now in the darkness follows me.

# The Afterlife

*Oh shabti allotted to me, if I be summoned or if I be detailed
to do any work which has to be done in the realm of the
dead...you shall detail yourself for me on every occasion of
making arable the fields, of flooding the banks or conveying
sand from east to west; 'Here am I,' you shall say.*

*– Book of the Dead*

1.

They're looking a little parched
after millennia standing side
by side in the crypt, but the limestone
Egyptian couple, inseparable
on their slab, emerge from it as noble
and grand as you could ask of people
thirteen inches tall.

The pleasant, droopy-breasted wife
smiles hospitably in her gown
(the V-necked sheath "a style popular
for the entire 3,000-year
Pharaonic period").
Her skin is painted paler than his:
a lady kept out of the sun.
Bare-chested in his A-line kilt,
her husband puts his spatulate
best foot forward, so as to stride
into a new life.

Not mummies; more like dummies.
Not idols, yet not merely dolls.
Stocky synecdoches
of the ruling class, they survey
an entourage of figurines
at work providing necessaries
for long days under the reigns
of dynasties still unborn.

To serenade them, here's a harpist.
A dwarf even in life –
a mascot to amuse the court
whose music must not be cut short.
A potter modeling vessels that seem,
like him, already fired in a kiln.
Six silos of wheat,
imaginary granaries.
A woman of stone grinding grain,
as she would have, on a quern of stone.
A woman winnowing grain in a pan.
Another on her knees, kneading.
A brewer mashing a vat of beer,
a butcher slitting the throat
of a heifer for the hereafter.


   2.

What had it felt like, that credence
in the afterlife of art?
To die, as the departed did,
comforted by the guaranteed
incarnation of a statuette;
to feed then on that slaughtered meat?

To take a leap from the stock-still
tyranny of the literal?
To see the miniature, the fiction
as a grow-in-the-dark depiction
of the soon-to-be actual?


   3.

Aboveground, thought was evolving.
So many lords and ladies died;

not everyone could be supplied
with a finely sculpted retinue
of laborers to keep them living.

And how were the high ones to keep
so many minions at their task?
The overseer with his whip
became a smiling, bland convention:
one foreman for every ten or so
farmers with a hoe.

It wasn't only math.
Something unforeseen
was undermining transfiguration –
a canny, efficient faith
that less detail might well stand in
for the stand-in;
a simplicity of encryption.

Hundreds and hundreds of years passed.
Alabaster, faience, wood,
the scale of the factotum totems
dwindled as numbers multiplied;
jostled in the mass graves
of toy-box coffins, they were transported
by a procession of living slaves
a little distance, and slipped
into their niches in the crypt
for the shelf-life of eternity.

Thumb-sized effigies wrapped
in bandages of holy script,
the hieroglyphed *Book of the Dead*.

Words. The nominal vow to work,
not the enactment of work.
The *shabti* held one stylized tool,
barely identifiable –
and were serene as Christian saints
with their hatchets and wheels, the instruments
of a recurring martyrdom.
In time they grew more mummiform,
cross-armed at the chest
or armless. Finally, curiously, at rest –

like zeroes who were something
in being nothing,
place-markers of their own
as much as of the master's soul.


   4.
And on the wall of a vault,
an artist has drawn himself –
or a cunning substitute –
at work, shaping a life-sized *shabti*
designed to be his twin:
a goateed dandy that our mute,
vainglorious ventriloquist
settles on one knee.

Profile to profile, they stare
into the mannered mirror
of one another.

In whatever kingdom this was
(by now, the blink
of one kohl-lined, almond eye),
what did people think was the lifespan

of the stunt man who betokens man?
The *shabti* sent to make *shabti*?

But the question too has shrunken,
eroded to vocabulary –
one fine old potsherd of a word
to be carried from the museum
like any other item
in the museum shop:
a replica necklace, a postcard.

The visitor is illiterate.
What did that stone scroll say,
meant to convert someday
to the thing it represents, papyrus?
Even the scribes couldn't read.
Something about the god Osiris
who came back from the dead.

She must be going.
Feels for the gloves in her pockets,
empty hands for her hands.

Opens a door to Chicago,
where a fine dust is ticking
coldly onto everything;
where she is still alive, and it's snowing.

# It's Hard to Say

That's what you say a hundred times a day.
        Yet we keep asking.
("How was your morning? Did you like the nurse?")
The worse you get, the louder we keep asking –
as though, if you heard better, you could say.

Two adjectives bob up sometimes, depending.
        Good things you call "amazing."
("How was the garden? Did you like the birds?")
Things are either "terrible" or "amazing."
Nothing is in the middle. It's the ending,

the drawn-out ending, of your verbal life.
        "It's hard to say,"
you say, as though by thinking you'd remember
your sentence: word by word, still less to say.
This man here is your son. I am his wife,

and it is, indeed, terrible and amazing
        you must be told again.
I know *you*, though – that undimmed politesse
of eighty-plus years when, awestruck again
by a too-brilliant question, you sit there gazing

thoughtfully into space, and only then
do you say the terrible thing. "It's hard to say."

# Over and Out

Ladies and gentlemen, this is your captain speaking.
Those of you on the left side of the aisle
surely have spotted, on this fine Fourth of July,
fireworks erupting all around the city.
Pockets of color. Ooh baby, look at that.
From thirty thousand feet, you never hear
the *pop pop* when they open. No, they seem
to blossom in the dark, in suspended silence –
to dilate and fill like delicate parachutes
descending with curious tautness, until at last
they safely resolve to a shimmer of memory
that lingers like stars, then truly disappears.
Or that's what I'm seeing. Excuse the poetry.
Sometimes I get carried away up here.
I've left the seatbelt sign illuminated,
and though we expect no turbulence, weather-wise,
I'll ask you not to move about the cabin
unless you have to. The truth is we're in trouble.
Those of you on the right side may have noted
a funny rumble. That's not the fireworks, folks.

I'm going to get this plane down the best I can.
I bet you'd trade in every one of your frequent
flier points for the real-life parachutes
we lack on this particular budget aircraft.
Wouldn't it be divine if we all drifted
to terra firma guided as if by winged
angels in parti-colored, ballooning silks?
Instead I'm duty-bound to propose that you
gather up – not your personal belongings
but any final reflections you may feel
will comfort you. Naturally you hate
being reminded your fate is in the hands
of faceless authority – that would be me;
but my advice is, try to rise above that.

You should have had a third little flask of scotch,
some of you are thinking. Some of you gals
are wishing our steward Keith, in business class,
so handsome, were available for a few
minutes, anyway. Triumphant sex
with strangers as the fireworks fade forever –

the dizzy thrill of The End? That dream would only
come true in the pathetic paperbacks
you brought onboard. Real terror, let me tell you,
is no aphrodisiac. How stupidly
you lined up for this trip! How much you cared
who was pre-boarded first, or whether Misty,
our blonde in coach, would start from the front or back
when she rolled out her little tinkling cart
of snack-boxes which, although not fit for a dog,
you paid for meekly, and with the exact change.

Let's be frank. This flight is headed for
your longest vacation. Tonight, the only gates
we'll taxi to are pearly: no connection
to the party raging on down there without us.
It's far too late to squander precious seconds
resenting my sadly true banalities,
my jocular despair, my loud, phoned-in
philosophy no button can switch off.
I understand, though. You'd like a little peace
before the eternal one. Well, here you are.
Spend your last moments in big-hearted hope
we're going to hurt nobody on the ground.

# No Second Try

*Why should I blame her that she filled my days*
*With misery…*

       – W. B. Yeats, "No Second Troy"

Why should I blame him that he filled his days
With mistresses, or that he came home late
To meet most ignorant trust with smiling ways,
Such thoughtful gifts, and claims that I looked great –
Whatever that meant, though clearly not desire?
What help if I'd been wiser, with a mind
Simply to hurl his laundry in the fire
Rather than buy his tall tales with a kind
Solicitude and a deluded kiss,
Having cleaned his house from stem to stern?
Why, who else could he use, a guy like this?
Was there another wife for him to spurn?

# String of Pearls

The pearls my mother gave me as a bride
rotted inside.
Well, not the pearls, but the string.
One day I was putting
them on, about thirty years on,
and they rattled onto the floor, one by one …
I'm still not sure I found them all.

As it happened, I kept a white seashell
on my vanity table. It could serve as a cup
where, after I'd scooped the lost pearls up,
I'd save them, a many-sister
haven in one oyster.
A female's born with all her eggs,
unfolds her legs,

then does her dance, is lovely, is the past –
is old news as the last
crinkle-foil-wrapped sweet
in the grass of the Easter basket.
True? Who was I? Had I unfairly classed
myself as a has-been? In the cloister
of the ovary, when

released by an extra dose of estrogen,
my chances for love dwindled, one by one.
But am I done?

# Complaint for Absolute Divorce

A little something to endorse:
*Download attachment, print and sign*
*Complaint for Absolute Divorce,*

the lawyer wrote with casual force.
Yet why complain? The suit was mine.
A little something to endorse

"Complaint": sheer poetry, of course,
more lofty than Lament or Whine.
Complaint for Absolute Divorce:

so well-phrased, who could feel remorse?
That "Absolute" was rather fine.
A little something to endorse

the universe as is: for worse,
for better. Nothing by design.
Complaint for Absolute Divorce,

let me salute you, sole recourse!
I put my birth-name on the line –
a little something – and endorse
the final word, then, in "Divorce."

# Bed of Letters

Propped like a capital
letter at the head
of what was once our bed,

or like a letterhead –
as if your old address
were printed on my face –

I'm writing you this note
folded in sheets you lay
on then, but sleeplessly

night after night, a man
whose life became about
the fear of being found out.

Rarely a cross word
between us, although today
I see the printer's tray

of your brain, the dormant type
sorted in little rooms
to furnish anagrams,

fresh headlines, infinite
new stories in nice fonts.
*Give her what she wants*,

you must have thought, and brought
home seedlings to transplant
in flowerbeds, unmeant

to bloom into such tall
tales – which even you
can't unsay or undo.

And yet it's true that long
ago, two lovers dozed
naked and enclosed

one history between covers.
We woke and, shy and proud,
read our new poems aloud.

# The Seafarer

*A version from the Anglo-Saxon*

I can sing my own true story
of journeys through this world,
how often I was tried
by troubles. Bitterly scared,
I would be sick with sorrow
on my night watch as I saw
so many times from the prow
terrible, tall waves
pitching close to cliffs.
My feet were frozen stiff,
seized and locked by frost,
although my heart was hot
from a host of worries.
A hunger from within
tore at my mind, sea-weary.

But men on solid ground
know nothing of how a wretch
like me, in so much pain,
could live a winter alone,
exiled, on the ice-cold sea
where hail came down in sheets,
and icicles hung from me
while friendly hall-companions
feasted far away.
The crashing sea was all
I heard, the ice-cold wave.
I made the wild swan's song
my game; sometimes the gannet
and curlew would cry out
though elsewhere men were laughing;
and the sea-mew would sing
though elsewhere men drank mead.

Storms beat against the stone
cliffs, and the ice-feathered
tern called back, and often
the sea-sprayed eagle too.

No kinsman can console
or protect a sorry soul.
In fact, a city dweller
who revels and swills wine
far from travel's perils
barely could believe
how often, wearily,
I weathered the sea paths.
The shadows of night deepened,
snow fell from the north,
and on the frost-bound earth
hail fell like the coldest grain.
For all that, my heart's thoughts
pound now with the salt
wave's surging; on high seas
my spirit urges me
forward, to seek far
from here a foreign land.

The truth is that no man –
however generous
in gifts, however bold
in youth, however brave,
however loyally
his own lord may attend him –
is ever wholly free
in his seafaring from worry
at what is the Lord's will.

No, it is not for him,
the harp's song, nor the rings
exchanged, nor pleasure in women,
nor any worldly glory,
nothing but welling waves;
the longing of seagoing
man is what he has.
Groves break into blossom,

the towns and fields grow fair
and the world once more is new:
all of this spurs on
the man whose mind and spirit
are eager for the journey,
who yearns to steer his course
far across the sea.

Mournfully the cuckoo's
voice cries out in warning,
the harbinger of summer
bitterly foretells
in song the soul's distress.
To the wealthy warrior
blessed with worldly fortune,
this is all unknown –
what we face who follow
the vast and alien way.

And now my thought roams far
beyond my heart; my mind
flows out to the water,
soars above the whale's path
to the wide world's corners
and returns with keen desire;
the lone bird, flying, shrieks

and leads the willing soul
to the whale-road, and over
the tumbling of the waves.

The joys of the Lord can kindle
more in me than dead
and fleeting life on land.
I do not believe the riches
of this world will last forever.
Always, without fail,
of three things one will turn
uncertain for a man
before his fatal hour:
sickness, age, or the sword
will rip the life right out
of the doomed and done for.
So it is for every man:
the best praise will come after,

from people who outlive him;
today, then, he must toil
against enemies and the Devil;
undaunted he must dare
so that sons of men extol him,
that in time to come his fame
endures amid the angels,
and his glory goes on, ceaseless,
among the celestial hosts.

The days are dwindling now
of the kingdoms of this earth;
there are no kings or Caesars
as before, and no gold-givers
as once, when men of valor
performed great deeds and lived

majestically among
themselves in high renown.
Their delights too are dead.
The weakest hold the world
in their hands, and wear it out
with labor, while all splendor,
like the earth, grows older;
its noble aspect withers
as man does everywhere.

Age creeps up on him,
his face grows pale; his head,
gray-haired, bewails old friends,
sons of princes, already
given to the earth.
As his body fails,
life leaks away, he tastes
sweetness in things no more,
nor feels pain, nor can move
his hand, nor use his mind.
When a kinsman dies, he wants
to strew the grave with gold,
or bury with the dead
treasures he amassed.
But no, it cannot be;
gold once hid and hoarded
in life is no good now
for the soul full of sin
before the force of God.

Terrible and great
is the Lord, and the very world
turns from Him in awe.
He made the firm foundations,
the earth's face and the heavens.

Foolish is he who does not fear
his Lord; death comes to him
though he is unprepared.
Blessed is he who lives in all
humility; what comes to him
in Heaven is forgiveness.
God gave to him that spirit
to bow to all His power.
A man must steer his passions,
be strong in staying steady;
keep promises, be pure.
He must be wise and fair
with foes as much as friends,
well-tempered in himself.
He dreads to see a dear one
engulfed in flames, yet patience
tells him to trust the sway
of Fate, and that God's might
is greater than we know.

Let us ponder where our true
home is, and how to reach it.
Let us labor to gain entry
into the eternal,
to find the blessedness
of belonging to the Lord
joyfully on high.
Thanks be to God who loved us,
the endless Father, the Prince
of Glory forever. Amen.

# Lost Originals

*All his life he spoke of 'lost originals,' as if he were reaching beyond his own civilization to the simplicity and grandeur of a remote past ...*

– Peter Ackroyd, *Blake*

The window to the mortal world
shows mountain islands in the sea.
One of them rises at the same
slope the soul floats from the body

flat on the bed, in stony folds,
the profiled head propped on a pillow.
A second distant hill has curled
into a corner of the window

(more a mirror than a window)
precisely in the size and shape
of the other pillow at the foot
of the bed from which, now flying up

from feet of clay, utterly free,
the female soul looks down on man,
her weeping hair a kind of pity,
her breasts as round as sun and moon.

\*

For a pittance he would illustrate
the poems of others, like *The Grave*
by Robert Blair (forgotten now,
of the graveyard school). He would engrave

a scene like this to make ends meet,
or sometimes furnish a first sketch
for wretches like that Schiavonetti –
who wrecked this one, and couldn't etch –

but beauty in the end was his,
for right was left, and black was white,
the world was flat and he went round
his cottage blessed with second sight,

like Catherine, his better half,
and when the visions would forsake
both of them, "What do we do then, Kate?"
"We kneel down and pray, Mr. Blake."

    *

Soul peeled like a printer's proof
off the body's copper plate.
Hands black as a chimneysweep's
worked and with black hands he ate.

Raging at injustices
to all of humankind, yet placid,
steady with needle, burin, paint,
he brushed the pastel tones with acid.

The worldly took their patronage
elsewhere when he made them wait
for pages queerly old and new,
ahead of their time, and always late.

Time was of such little note!
Heaven came by *the infernal
method, corrosives, which in Hell
are salutary and medicinal;*

birds sang their eternal song
and angels lodged beneath his roof.
Off the body's copper plate
soul peeled like a printer's proof.

    *

Illuminations like stained glass
on paper, or like parasols
that shaded with a pale translucence;
enlightenment from Paracelsus

himself, beloved sage, who said
*imagination is like the sun:*
*its light, intangible, may set*
*a house afire.* O let light in

from deities of every source –
the New and the Old Testament,
gods of the Greeks, the Romans, Norse,
gods of *wise heathens*, gods that went

so many eons back he had
to invent them, so to mourn their loss.
Saturated colors sang
prophecies. In *The Song of Los*

he burned the institutions, *Churches:*
*Hospitals: Castles: Palaces:*
(built, he wrote, *like nets & gins*
*& traps to catch the joys*

*of Eternity)* on a treated plate
and turned it, coining true from false.
"All his life," the future wrote,
"he spoke of 'lost originals.'"

    \*

London turned meanwhile, cog-wheeled
industry of speed; grinding
people up in mills, it spilled
William Blake on common ground.

Rest in peace, white chalk and red,
hammer and chisel, rest in peace,
aqua fortis, vinegar,
salad oil, and candle grease.

No gravestone for the great engraver.
Never mind. We'll meet hereafter.
Catherine, who'd lost her beauty
to toil and hunger years before,

had posed a last time (*you have ever
been an angel to me*), and
sold his works to stay alive.
Let the future understand

he sat with her for hours together
daily following his death,
and she followed his instructions
from Jerusalem or Lambeth,

Bunhill Fields, Soho or Felpham,
Fountain Court, all was the same –
and soul, its twisted sheets in tatters,
rose up from its bed of letters.

# A Note About the Author

Mary Jo Salter was born in Grand Rapids, Michigan, and grew up in Detroit and Baltimore. She was educated at Harvard and Cambridge and worked as a staff editor at *The Atlantic Monthly* and as poetry editor of *The New Republic*. In addition to her seven previous poetry collections, she is the author of a children's book, *The Moon Comes Home*, a coeditor of *The Norton Anthology of Poetry*, and is a playwright and lyricist. After many years of teaching at Mount Holyoke College in South Hadley, Massachusetts, she is now Krieger-Eisenhower Professor in The Writing Seminars at Johns Hopkins University in Baltimore, Maryland.

# Other Books from Waywiser

*Other Books from Waywiser*

Clive Watkins, *Already the Flames*
Clive Watkins, *Jigsaw*
Richard Wilbur, *Anterooms*
Richard Wilbur, *Mayflies*
Richard Wilbur, *Collected Poems 1943-2004*
Norman Williams, *One Unblinking Eye*
Greg Williamson, *A Most Marvelous Piece of Luck*

### Fiction
Gregory Heath, *The Entire Animal*
Mary Elizabeth Pope, *Divining Venus*
K. M. Ross, *The Blinding Walk*
Gabriel Roth, *The Unknowns**
Matthew Yorke, *Chancing It*

### Illustrated
Nicholas Garland, *I wish ...*
Eric McHenry and Nicholas Garland, *Mommy  Daddy  Evan  Sage*

### Non-Fiction
Neil Berry, *Articles of Faith: The Story of British Intellectual Journalism*
Mark Ford, *A Driftwood Altar: Essays and Reviews*
Richard Wollheim, *Germs: A Memoir of Childhood*

* Co-published with Picador